# Change

Jon-Arild Johannessen

Copyright © 2016 Jon-Arild Johannessen

All rights reserved.

ISBN: 1535591625
ISBN-13: 9781535591621

DEDICATION


To my wife

# CONTENTS

## Part I Theory .................................................................................. 1
### Chapter 1 Prospect Theory ........................................................ 2
Introduction .......................................................................................... 2
Decision-making under uncertainty..................................................... 4
Heuristic assessments ........................................................................ 15
Specific measures that management can implement....................... 22
Decision-making under uncertainty................................................... 22
Framing ............................................................................................... 23
Heuristic assessments ........................................................................ 25
Conclusion........................................................................................... 27
References.......................................................................................... 30

## Part II Understanding Change .................................................. 35
### Chapter 2 Social mechanisms for change .................................. 36
Introduction ........................................................................................ 36
Social mechanisms ............................................................................. 39
Social mechanisms and explanation models..................................... 43
Elaborating on social mechanisms and causal relations in social systems................................................................................................ 48
Historical causal processes and social mechanisms........................ 51
Functional causal processes and social mechanisms...................... 52
Cybernetic causal processes and social mechanisms ..................... 54
Pattern processes and social mechanisms....................................... 56
Elaborating on social mechanisms and pattern processes.......... 59
Social mechanisms, models and theories ........................................ 63
Conclusion........................................................................................... 71
References.......................................................................................... 73

## Part III Explaining change ........................................................ 79
### Chapter 3 Institutional changes ................................................ 80
Introduction ........................................................................................ 80
Explaining institutional change .......................................................... 82
Explaining institutional change: A historical perspective............. 84
Explaining institutional change: A cybernetic perspective .......... 87
Explaining institutional change: A functional perspective ........... 92

Explaining institutional change: A pattern perspective ............... 95
Conclusion .................................................................................. 98
Referenses ............................................................................... 101

# Part IV Change in society ................................................. 108
## Chapter 4 Change from industrial society to knowledge society ....................................................................................... 109
Introduction ............................................................................. 109
Infostructure ........................................................................... 120
Front line focus ....................................................................... 125
Modular flexibility .................................................................. 130
Global competence clusters ..................................................... 133
Conclusion .............................................................................. 139
References .............................................................................. 141

# Chapter on concepts ........................................................ 152
# Index ................................................................................ 182
THE AUTHOR ........................................................................ 186

# Part I Theory

## Chapter 1 Prospect Theory

Introduction

The problem under investigation is people's resistance to organizational change (Griffin & Moorhead, 2014; Harvey, 2010; Evans, 2001). This chapter investigates the following question: How can prospect theory be used to explain why people resist organizational change? The chapter aims to identify how managers can reduce resistance to change. It also aims to identify explanations of why people resist organizational change. The key concept of this investigation is how people relate to particular risks that they are experiencing.

Risk relates to our assumptions about potential outcomes and how these outcomes are evaluated by the decision-maker(s) in question (Pollatsek & Tversky, 1970, p. 541; Elster, 1986). Prospect theory was developed by Kahneman and Tversky in 1979 (Kahneman & Tversky, 1979). The theory holds that when people are faced with a risk about which they have limited information, and do not apply rigorous analytical processes, their choices will often be driven by how the information about the situation is framed either by themselves or others (Wolfe, 2008, p. 6).

The core idea of prospect theory is that people make assessments based on what they may gain or lose as the result of making a choice. One example of such a choice might be whether or not to engage actively in a change process within an organization. According to prospect theory, the possibility of losing an existing position will generate a level of resistance that will outweigh the energy and resources a person might expend in order to gain a new position (Kahneman, 2011, pp. 279-280). Most people are averse to losing something that they have already gained.

People's assessments are largely biased, distorted and not wholly reliable. Regardless of this fact, people make considerable use of these assessments in decision-making. Tversky and Kahneman found in the course of the research that led them to develop prospect theory that these assessments were heuristics or "rules of thumb" that people use in decision-making (Tversky & Kahneman, 1974, 1983). A basic assumption in prospect theory is that people use these rules of thumb without even realizing that they are doing so. The content of this chapter is summarized in Fig. 1, which also shows how the chapter is structured. This chapter also includes a separate section that explains concrete measures that may be taken by management. These measures are based on the seven propositions developed during the course of this chapter.

Fig. 1: Prospect theory as an explanation of why people resist organizational change.

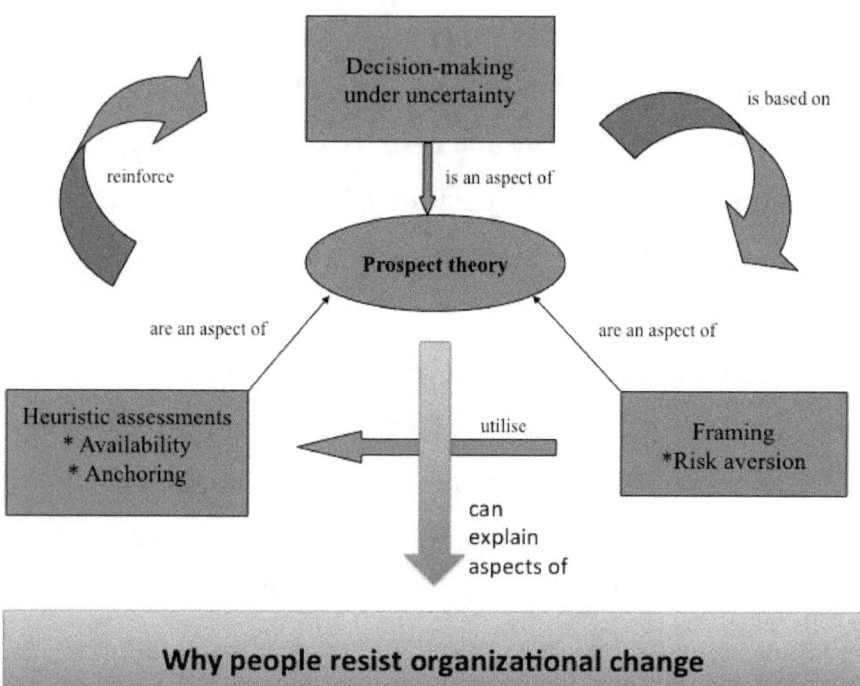

### Decision-making under uncertainty

At first, it may seem reasonable to assume that people will seek out risk if they are living under poor conditions. This assumption concludes that the situation can't get worse, so people will take risks in order to improve their life situation.

According to prospect theory, however, this intuitive assumption is incorrect. In fact, when a person faces the possibility of losing the rights, power, positions, income, etc., that he or she has already achieved, they will seek to retain what they have achieved and are reluctant to change (Kahneman & Tversky, 2000, p. 22). People avoid participating in change processes for as long as possible because they risk losing what they have achieved.

The explanation of why people are risk-averse is linked to what is known in prospect theory as the "certainty effect" (Kahneman & Tversky, 2000, p. 17). Very broadly, this effect can be described as a preference for the certain over the possible.

What is different about prospect theory, in contrast to, for example, rational choice theory (Kahneman, 2011), is that prospect theory takes account of how we will act both when we face the loss of rights, positions, etc., and when we face the possibility of gaining the same kinds of rights, positions, etc. If one is in a situation where one risks losing positions one has gained, one will be willing to take a risk in order to retain one's current position. If one faces a situation where one has an expectation of gain, then the probability is great (paradoxically) that one will prefer to secure what one has already achieved.

Prospect theory uses the phrase "reference point" to denote the point at which we take action in the various situations described above. Our assessment of a situation is determined by the position we are in when we undertake the process of assessing the situation. The key psychological concept of prospect theory is that people dislike the idea of losing a position but like the idea of winning one (Kahneman, 2011, p. 281). The important point here, however, is that people will commit more effort to preventing a loss than achieving a potential gain (Kahneman & Tversky, 2000, p. 22). In addition, Kahneman and Tversky state that people's commitment increases when they are trying to prevent a loss but decreases when they are trying to gain something (Kahneman & Tversky, 2000, p. 17). For all practical purposes, this means that the energy and resources a person will use to prevent a loss will increase in proportion to the likely size of the loss. The converse is not true in respect of a gain.

**Proposition 1.** If management structures their change project to take account of the fact that people will resist change because they risk losing what they have already achieved, then the change project will have a greater chance of success.

**Practical implications.** People will expend more energy and resources on preventing losses than on gaining new positions.

**Management implications.** Management should be aware

that if employees face a situation that offers a potential benefit then the likelihood is great that they will prefer instead to secure their existing positions.

The "reflection effect" reverses the "certainty effect". As a rule of thumb, resistance to change is reversed when the possible gains are between 1.5 and 2.5 times greater than the status quo (Kahneman, 2011, p. 284). It is when gains reach this point that participation in organizational changes comes into consideration. This concerns when one can choose between retaining that which is established and secure on the one hand, and investing resources in a process of change on the other. The choice will, in the context of the "reflection effect", be related to the expectation of future opportunities to choose to participate in change, rather than to retaining a reliable and proven solution.

A third psychological effect that prospect theory refers to is the "isolation effect" (Kahneman & Tversky, 2000, p. 17). This refers to people's tendency to discard elements that all choice situations have in common, leading to inconsistent preferences. The focus in this context is on what separates the choice options, i.e. that which creates a distinction (Tversky, 1972). Among other things, this effect means that choice options are broken down and framed in terms of a probability of loss or possibility of gain. If a change situation is presented as involving a probable loss, then one will maintain the status quo. However, if the change is presented as an opportunity to make very large gains, say more than 100 per cent of what one already has, then it will be possible to apply the certainty effect and the reflection effect to move someone from a status quo situation to a situation involving investment and commitment to a change project. Presenting information in this way means that people are willing to change, even if they do not have complete information about the outcome.

Fig. 2 shows a model of how the three effects (certainty effect, reflection effect and isolation effect) can vary in relation to each other, explaining resistance to change during organizational changes.

Fig. 2: Resistance to change in organizations.

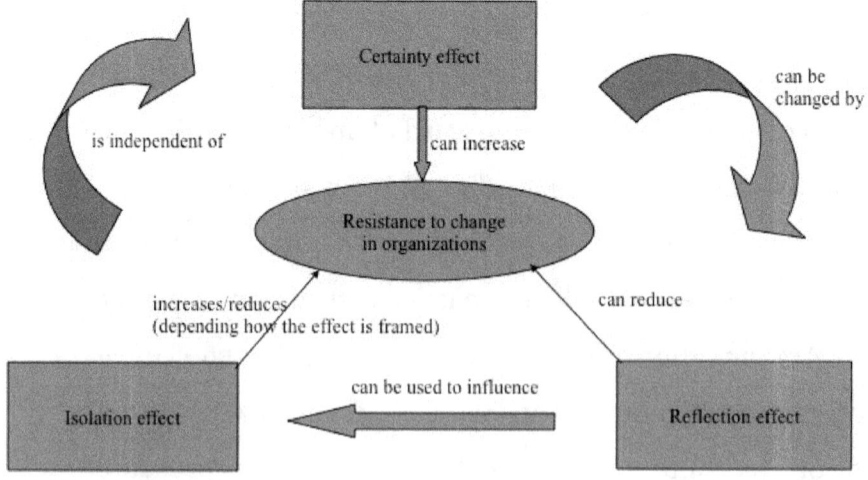

In prospect theory, psychological assessments are related to three elements: losing, winning and the reference point (McDermott, 2001). The reference point is, as a rule, related to expectations or the status quo (Kahneman, 2011, p. 282). What is perceived by some as a large gain may be perceived by others as insignificant (Vis, 2010).

In prospect theory, there is always a reference point related to expectations about a possible gain. This is the basis for assessing whether to seek to secure what you already have or to seek any changes that present themselves.

The practical choices are often complex and involve a risk of loss and a possibility of gain. Consequently, we operate, in effect, with a subjective assessment of expected usefulness in relation to our choices. There are risks and uncertainties associated with choices: the choices are often not that clear-cut and frequently include mixed assessments.

A useful rule of thumb for managers that can encourage people to engage in an organizational change project is to be aware that the expected gains must be about 100 per cent or more in relation to the status quo. The tendency will then be to choose the option for potential gains in spite of the fact that there is still the possibility of loss (Vis, 2010). Experiments have shown that the rate of loss aversion increases with increasing investment, so the more that is at stake, the greater the possibility of gain must also be if one is to choose to fully embark on a change project (McDermott, 2001). However, the loss aversion rate does not increase proportionally with the possibility of loss. For instance, in situations where life is threatened or people are exposed to bankruptcy, the degree of loss aversion is dramatically high. There are certain actions that are unacceptable no matter what the possible final gain (Kahneman, 2011, p. 284). This may explain why some people enter into organizational change processes while others don't. In practice, the degree of loss aversion can be much greater for some people depending on their life experiences (Vis, 2010). For instance, individuals and groups accustomed to experiencing losses, such as professional gamblers, military officers, financial brokers, vulnerable and marginalized groups, etc., may have a greater tolerance of losses.

**Proposition 2.** If management presents the changes as an opportunity to achieve a gain of more than 100 per cent of what employees already have (the status quo), then it is highly probable that employees will consider the change project as positive.

**Practical implications.** If management wants to reduce resistance to change, then they should present the possible gain as being more than 100 per cent.

**Management implications.** Management can reduce resistance to change in organizations by taking advantage of the interaction between the certainty effect, the reflection effect, and the isolation effect.

Framing

Prospect theory assumes that people do not act on the basis of full information when making decisions. They instead usually act on the basis of available information. Following from this, the theory does *not* assume that people are fully rational when making choices. The theory investigates how people act in practice when making choices, asking, for example, how they use intuition when making choices in uncertain situations. When faced with a choice between an uncertain change that may offer future opportunities and a current status quo situation, people often act on the basis of the proverb "A bird in the hand is worth two in the bush". In other words, we tend to choose the safe option over the one which is uncertain but which offers opportunities.

Some people also tend to be optimistic about any given situation they find themselves in. Such a bias is both a blessing and a risk, says Kahneman (Kahneman, 2011, p. 255). The so-called "pessimists" and "optimists" have been examined and discussed in several empirical studies (Seligman, 2006; Snowdon, 2001; Fox, Ridgewell, & Ashwin, 2009). The optimists, Kahneman writes, are "…the inventors, the entrepreneurs. ...They got to where they are by seeking challenges and taking risks" (Kahneman, 2011, p. 256). Although most of us are risk-averse, some of us are optimists and willing to participate in change processes even though expectations do not offer 100 per cent or greater gains regarding the possible outcome.

**Proposition 3.** If management discovers who the optimists are and assigns them to the change project, then the probability is great that the change project will succeed.

**Practical implications.** We tend to opt for that which is established and safe and discard the opportunity for potential gains. This conservative element in human decision-making may also partly explain why there is a time lag between an assumed necessary change and the impact of change in the organization.

**Management implications.** It is easier to involve the optimists in a change project than the pessimists. Management should therefore search for optimists and let them be the agents of change for the project.

It is the framing aspect of prospect theory that has received most attention (Wolfe, 2008, p. 9). Framing can be understood as the way in which "individuals and groups make sense of their external environment" (Boettcher, 2004, p. 331). We use framing to organize and understand the world around us.

Using information frames, we are able to perceive a phenomenon, issue, event, etc., in a new way. Prospect theory argues that framing is used to make choices and assumptions in relation to future outcomes (Tversky & Kahneman, 1981). How information concerning our choices is presented is an important consideration in the framing phase of prospect theory (McDermott, 2001, p. 21). We can also frame that which is rational so that it appears reasonable, even though something that is rationally justified might not necessarily have a reasonable justification. Sense and rationality can be contradictory terms, although they may also be congruent. The most general part of framing in prospect theory concerns how a loss is framed in relation to a gain. This may be achieved by selecting information frames that result in the loss or gain appearing in a different light to an individual.

Losses and gains are considered in relation to the status quo and what will serve one's own interests or those of the system (Mandel, 2001). The framing or editing of a given situation may be termed prospect theory's initial phase (McDermott, 2001, p. 20). In many situations we are not aware of what opportunities exist or the possible outcomes of our choices. Consequently, we often construct possible alternatives and the results of pursuing them before making a decision; this is the creative aspect in any decision-making process. It is during this stage that management should think through the importance of which information frames they will use. In other words, according to prospect theory we adopt a kind of bias. We have an aversion to losing what we have already gained; therefore, our choices will be influenced by how the choices and the prospective results of these choices are framed. How the information framework is used is consequently not an insignificant part of the outcome of how people react to change projects in organizations.

Tversky and Kahneman express this clearly by saying that "...choice depends on the status quo, or reference level: changes of reference point lead to reversals of preference" (Tversky & Kahneman, 2000, p. 143). In our context, this can explain the importance of how information frameworks are presented in relation to the extent of resistance to change in organizations.

One of the principal assumptions of prospect theory that emphasizes the importance of information frames is that "losses and disadvantages have greater impact on preferences than gains and advantages" (Tversky & Kahneman, 2000, p. 143). Loss aversion in prospect theory has major implications for how people in organizations relate to change and how their preferences change when reference points shift over time. Information frames are concerned with moving the reference point, not providing valid information that is completely reliable.

**Proposition 4.** If management frames information concerning the change project as representing a large gain for everyone, then the probability is great that employees will consider the change project in a positive light.

**Practical implications.** The assumption here is that it is people's perception of the reference point that will move them in one direction or the other.

**Management implications.** Management should be cautious about introducing too many changes simultaneously and carrying out rapid changes in succession because this may easily lead to erratic behavior in organizations. This can lead to a loss of efficiency and increased resistance to change projects in the organization.

## Heuristic assessments

There are four basic heuristic assessments that Tversky and Kahneman have described (Beach & Connolly, 2005, pp. 81-83; Kahneman, 2011; Tversky & Kahneman, 1974, 1983). These are:

1. Representativeness and randomness,
2. Anchoring
3. Availability
4. Validity.

In this chapter, only anchoring and availability will be discussed because these are the most relevant in explaining why people oppose change in organizations.

## Anchoring.

A boat at anchor can move around, but the anchorage will always be its pivot point. To move the anchor point, you have to take up the anchor and physically move it to another place. If you have first dropped anchor, then you have also chosen the pivot point or the point around which negotiations will revolve. The anchor effect does not concern a lack of or incorrect information; it is an effect that seems to apply even if we have sufficient information (Chapman & Johnson, 2002). When we are trying to estimate something, such as the probable success of a change project, the development of property prices (Northcraft & Neale, 1987), the benefits of adopting a new idea in an organizational change project, etc., we will often begin by making an initial estimate. This is our so-called "anchor". We will then make adjustments in relation to the anchor (Beach & Connolly, 2005, pp. 82-83). However, if the anchor is not placed correctly, then the probability is great that the final results will also differ from what was originally planned. This calls to mind a popular quotation from Ibsen's *Peer Gynt*: "But when the starting point is weakest the result is often the most original".

Thus, according to prospect theory, where you set the anchor in relation to a prospect will affect subsequent behavior

(Kahneman, 2011, p. 119). Whether one chooses to invest in a change project is also related to the anchor of how project information is framed, i.e. the risk in relation to winning or losing what has already been gained. If you take the risk of investing in a change project, how much is the potential upside? We have seen above that the potential upside should be more than 100 per cent. However, experiments have also shown that the gain should range between as much as 150 and 250 per cent if one is to take the risk of investing in something new. It is the anchor related to risk aversion that is interesting from a change perspective, because it says something about how willing the individual is to engage in a change project.

An interesting aspect from an information perspective is that people consider their potential gains and losses from the anchor that has been set even when it has been set randomly (Chapman & Johnson, 2002:120-138). It appears that the anchor effect operates in such a way that the end result on average does not vary by more than 55 per cent from the anchor that was originally set. In experiments, this seems to apply even if the anchor is not taken into account (Kahneman, 2011:124). From an information perspective, this is important knowledge for management or those who are selling a change project.

An interesting point related to anchors is that they affect us, although we are aware of this (Wilson & Brekke, 1994:117-

142). Anchors are used to extract and select information, integrate this information and then formulate a response to another party (Chapman & Johnson, 2002, p. 126). This says something about the strength of the anchor effect.

**Proposition 5.** If management uses the anchor effect to control people's resistance to change, then the probability is great that employees will engage positively in the change project.

**Practical implications.** The anchor effect explains aspects of why people oppose changes in organizations and may be used to reduce people's resistance to change.

**Management implications.** Management should be aware of the fact that the anchor effect may differ by 55 per cent from a set anchor.

## Availability.

If information is available at regular intervals, then it is easy to refer to such information (Beach & Connolly, 2005, p. 82). We say in such situations that the information is available in one's memory. However, it is not only information that is often repeated that is available for retrieval in one's memory; events that have left a deep impression also have the same availability effect. For instance, emotional childhood experiences, air disasters, genocide, pestilence, economic crises, change projects that went wrong resulting in mass dismissals, etc., are easier to recall from memory than, for example, the fact that thousands of people are killed every year in traffic accidents.

It is therefore understandable that journalists, historians, and others compare the 2008 economic crisis with the 1930s depression because examples from the 1930s depression can easily be retrieved from memory. However, it is dangerous to make such a comparison if the 1930s depression can only to a small extent be relevantly compared to the 2008 economic crisis. If politicians initiate measures for the recent economic crisis on the basis of knowledge of initiatives that should have been adopted in the 1930s, this may create more problems than it solves. This example says something about the importance of information availability.

The question "Why do we believe more in one type of information than in another type?" may, among other things, be answered by the fact that some types of information are easier to retrieve from memory than others. In other words, the information we believe in is more "true" than other types of information. In this context, the expression "availability cascades" used by Kuran and Sunstein (Kuran & Sunstein, 1999) is of interest. By this they mean that we are to a certain extent controlled by the image of reality that is constructed by the media because it is easier to retrieve from memory. How easily information may be retrieved from memory when faced with a situation demonstrates the availability proposition's relevance. The availability proposition can be expressed in the following way: the more easily information enters into our consciousness, the greater the likelihood that we will have confidence in that information. In other words, we believe more in the type of information that is available in the memory than information that is not so readily available.

What is important to note concerning the availability proposition is that information does not necessarily need to be credible as long as it is available. It is, inter alia, in such contexts that Kahneman asks us to use System 2 (Kahneman, 2011), which he uses to refer to analytical thinking to check the validity of information. However, it is the availability proposition that prevails, because most people are not trained in statistics and analysis of information.

**Proposition 6.** If management uses the information available in the memory of employees and develops an anchor in relation to this information, then the probability is great that employees will consider the change project in a positive light. **Practical implications.** We have a tendency to distort information and believe that the information that is easier to retrieve from memory is more credible than information that emerges after thorough analysis.

***Management implications.*** Management should use information about change projects that can easily be compared with historical or contemporary events that employees can easily identify with.

A variation of the availability proposition is the affect proposition, which concerns how emotionally affected you are by the situation that is being assessed. In other words, the perceived risk of a project may be reduced if you are more emotionally affected by the project. In the real world, "we often face painful trade-offs between benefits and costs" (Kahneman, 2011, p. 140). Whether you choose to engage in a change project or prefer the status quo may depend on how emotionally affected you are by the project.

***Proposition 7.*** If management succeeds in getting employees emotionally involved in the change process, then the probability is great that they will consider the perceived risk associated with such changes as small.

***Practical implications.*** Whether people are willing to engage in a change project or try to preserve the status quo may depend on the extent to which they experience changes as emotionally attractive.

***Management implications.*** To increase the emotional reward of a change, it seems reasonable to assume that management should use the anchor effect and framing.

## Specific measures that management can implement

On the basis of the seven propositions described above, the following measures may be considered to reduce resistance to change in organizations.

### Decision-making under uncertainty
**Risk aversion.**

As a general rule, people seek to retain what they have already gained and are reluctant to change. We often operate on the basis of intuitive rules and psychological principles that govern the framing of information about our choices. However, these rules and principles are not necessarily rational or logical.

Management can apply this knowledge in order to reduce resistance to change by:

1. Crisis understanding: point out the necessity of the changes.
2. Psychological safety: point out that the proposed changes do not carry any risk of loss for employees.
3. Expectation management: point out the benefits of the changes.

**The potential must be more than 100 per cent.**

There are three effects that may be employed in efforts to reduce resistance to change in organizations. The first is called the "certainty effect". This implies that one chooses what is certain, i.e. what you already have, rather than that which is probable and offers opportunities, such as engaging in an organizational change project where the outcome is uncertain. The second effect is called the "reflection effect", which reverses the "certainty effect" if there are expectations of future gains of more than 100 per cent stemming from the change. The third effect is called the "isolation effect", which refers to a tendency to discard elements that all choices have in common and to focus on what separates the choices (Kahneman & Tversky, 2000, p. 17).

Management may increase the likelihood that employees will engage with and dedicate themselves to a change project by presenting the changes in such a way that they will lead to improvements in the proposition to employees that accrue to gains of more than 100 per cent across a number of change proposal elements.

## Framing

**We seek safety.**

We have a tendency to be conservative in our thinking: we wish to retain that which we have and are reluctant to adopt that which is new. One way for management to engage with this conservative aspect of our thinking may be to engage those who have little risk aversion in relation to the change project as project managers at various levels. The rationale for this strategy is provided by Kahneman. The people who are responsible for the implementation of a change project are often more optimistic than those who are not in this position, and optimists are more positive about change than pessimists. Kahneman underlines this supposition with the following statement: "…the people who have the greatest influence on the lives of others are likely to be optimistic and overconfident, and to take more risks than they realize" (Kahneman, 2011, p. 256).

Management should identify the optimists in the organization because they will most likely participate in the change project even though the possible future gain is not more than 100 per cent. They should also identify the sceptics to the change project and give them responsibility for some of the changes.

**Erratic behavior.**

If management introduces too many consecutive changes this can easily result in the organization becoming unsettled.

Consequently, employees may become reluctant to accept more changes. This may result in alienating those who initially supported the need for change and give more weight to those who are opposed to change.

Management may prevent such erratic behavior by involving employees at an early stage in the planning of changes. In the planning phase they should frame information so that the change project is presented as a win-win solution, where employees make large gains and risk losing little. In this way everyone is informed about what must be done, why it should be done, how it should be done, and the desired effects of the changes.

## Heuristic assessments
### Anchoring.

Use of the anchor effect for strategic purposes can result in us making choices we would not normally make. Countless experiments have shown that people's choices correspond to the anchor they use, even though the anchor may be irrelevant, random and evidently incorrectly set (Epley & Gilovich, 2002, p. 139). If you have a strong expectation of future success, then this expectation, this anchor, influences your behavior in the present (Switzer & Sniezek, 1991). Taking into account the anchor effect can help reduce resistance to change in organizations (Tversky & Kahneman, 1974). Moreover, it is advantageous to frame your project with a possible future gain of 150–250 per cent in relation to the status quo. An important point concerning the anchor effect is that it controls our behavior, even though we have sufficient information about the situation.Management can use this insight by setting the anchor in such a way that expectations are motivating for the individual.

**Availability.**

The availability proposition developed by Tversky and Kahneman in 1972–1973 (Kahneman, 2011, p. 129) can be expressed in the following simplified form: the easier information is to retrieve from memory, the greater the cognitive authority that information has. If you want to sell a change project, then it can be advantageous to link it to a media event that has a positive connotation.

Management can reduce resistance to change by linking the change project to a media event that has a strong positive connotation (cascade effect).

**Emotional strength.**

One relies more on information that reinforces our perception of the object, event or action if we are emotionally attracted to the object. When this happens we will take greater risks, and we will have a tendency to assign less importance to information that is critical and rely more on information that is positively charged in relation to the change project.

Management should encourage employees to become emotionally connected to the change project because this will trigger individual commitment and dedication to change.

## Conclusion

In this chapter we have attempted to answer the following question: how can we use prospect theory to explain why people resist organizational change? To answer this question seven propositions have been developed.

There are three magnitudes around which the propositions are organized. These are: decision-making under uncertainty, framing, and heuristic assessments (anchoring and availability).

In Decision-making under uncertainty there are two propositions. Proposition one is related to the knowledge that if people risk losing what they have already achieved, they will resist change. Proposition two says that the probability is high that employees will consider the change project as positive, if they think they achieve a gain of more than 100 per cent of what one already has (the status quo).

In Framing there are also two propositions. The first proposition in framing tells management to discovers who the optimists are, and assigns them to the change project. If they do so, then the probability is great that the change project will succeed. The second proposition in framing says that management ought to frame information concerning the change project as representing a large gain for everyone. If they do so, then the probability is great that employees will consider the change project in a positive light.

In Heuristic assessments there are three propositions in two categories: anchoring and availability. We have one proposition in Anchoring. This propositions states that if management uses the anchor effect to control people's resistance to change, then the probability is great that employees will engage positively with the change project.

We have two propositions in availability. The first proposition states that if management uses the information available in the memory of employees, and develops an anchor in relation to this information, then the probability is great that employees will consider the change project in a positive light.

The second proposition in availability tells that if management succeeds in getting employees emotionally involved in the change process, then the probability is great that they will consider the perceived risk associated with such changes as small.

Taken together the seven proposition have been compiled into a system, defined here as a "mini-theory", about how resistance to organizational change can be reduced. For each of the seven propositions we have discussed practical and management implications.

# References

Adriaenssen, D.J., & Johannessen, J-A. (2015). Conceptual generalisation: Methodological reflections in social science, a systemic viewpoint. *Kybernetes: The International Journal of Cybernetics, Systems and Management Sciences*,44,4:588-605.

Beach, L.R., & Connolly, T. (2005). *The psychology of decision making: People in organizations.* London: Sage.

Boettcher, W.A. (2004). The prospects for prospect theory: An empirical evaluation of international relations applications of framing and loss aversion. *Political Psychology, 25 (3)*, 331-362.

Bunge, M. (1974). *Sense and reference.* Dordrecht: Reidel.

Bunge, M. (1998). *Philosophy of science: From problem to theory: Vol. 1.* New Brunswick, NJ: Transaction.

Bunge, M. (1999). *The sociology-philosophy connection.* New Brunswick, NJ: Transaction.

Bunge, M. (2001). *Philosophy in crisis: The need for reconstruction.* Amherst, NY: Prometheus Books.

Chapman, G.B., & Johnson, E.J. (2002). Incorporating the irrelevant: Anchors in judgments of belief and value. In T. Gilovich, D. Griffin & D. Kahneman (Eds.), *Heuristics and biases:*

*The psychology of intuitive judgment* (pp. 120-138). Cambridge: Cambridge University Press.

Elster, J. (1986). *Rational choice.* New York: New York University Press.

Epley, N., & Gilovich, T. (2002). Putting adjustment back in the anchoring and adjustment heuristic. In T. Gilovich, D. Griffin & D. Kahneman (Eds.), *Heuristics and biases: The psychology of intuitive judgment* (pp. 139-149). Cambridge: Cambridge University Press.

Evans, R. (2001). *The human side of school change.* London: Jossey-Bass.

Fox, E., Ridgewell, A., & Ashwin, C. (2009). Looking on the bright side: Biased attention and the human serotonin transporter gene. *Proceedings of the Royal Society B, 276,* 1747-1751..

Griffin, R., & Moorhead, G. (2014). *Organizational behavior: Managing people and organizations* (pp. 543-546). Mason, OH: South Western Cengage Learning.

Harvey, T.R. (2010). *Resistance to change.* London: R & L Education.

Kahneman, D. (2011). *Thinking fast and slow.* New York: Allen Lane.

Kahneman, D., & Tversky, A. (1979). An analysis of decision under risk. *Econometrica, Journal of the Econometric Society, 47*(2), 263-292.

Kahneman, D., & Tversky, A. (2000). Prospect theory: An analysis of decision under risk. In D. Kahneman, & A. Tversky (Eds.), *Choices, values and frames* (pp. 17-43) Cambridge: Cambridge University Press.

Kuran, T., & Sunstein, C.R. (1999). Availabilities cascades and risk regulation. *Stanford Law Review, 51*, 683-768.

Mandel, D.R. (2001). Gain-loss framing and choice: Separating outcome formulations from descriptor formulations. *Organizational Behavior and Human Decision Processes, 85 (1)*, 56-76.

Northcraft, G.B., & Neale, M.A. (1987). Experts, amateurs, and real estate: An anchoring-and-adjustment perspective on property pricing decisions. *Organizational Behavior and Human Decision Processes, 39*, 84-97.

Pollatsek, A., & Tversky, A. (1970). A theory of risk. *Journal of Mathematical Psychology, 7*, 540-553.

Seligman, M.E.P. (2006). *Learned optimism*. New York: Vintage Books.

Snowdon, D. (2001). *Aging with grace: What the nun study*

*teaches us about leading longer, healthier, and more meaningful lives.* New York: Bantam Books.

Switzer, F., & Sniezek, J.A. (1991). Judgment processes in motivation: Anchoring and adjustment effects on judgment and behavior. *Organizational Behavior and Human Decision Processes, 49*, 208-229.

Tversky, A. (1972). Elimination by aspects: A theory of choice. *Psychological Review, 79*, 281-299.

Tversky, A., & Kahneman, D. (1974). Judgment under uncertainty: Heuristics and biases. *Science, 185*, 1124-1131.

Tversky, A., & Kahneman, D. (1981). The framing of decisions and the psychology of choice. *Science, 211*, 453-458.

Tversky, A., & Kahneman, D. (1983). Extensional versus intuitive reasoning. The conjunction fallacy in probability judgment. *Psychological Review, 90*, 293-315.

Tversky, A., & Kahneman, D. (2000). Loss aversion in riskless choice. In D. Kahneman, & A. Tversky (Eds.), *Choices, values and frames* (pp.143-158). Cambridge: Cambridge University Press.

Vis, B. (2010). *Politics of risk-taking* (pp. 109-133). Amsterdam: Amsterdam University Press.

Wilson, T.D. & Brekke, N. (1994). Mental contamination and

mental correction: Unwanted influences on judgment and evaluations. *Psychological Bulletin, 116*, 117-142.

Wolfe, W.M. (2008). *Winning the war of words*. London: Praeger.

# Part II Understanding Change

## Chapter 2 Social mechanisms for change

Introduction

In sociology the idea of social mechanisms was introduced to sociology by Merton (1967), even though rudiments can be detected both with Weber and protestant ethics explaining the growth of capitalism in Europe, and with Durkheim with the explanation of the increasing suicide rate. For Merton social mechanisms are building blocks for middle range theories. Merton (1968: 43) defines social mechanisms as "social processes having designated consequences for designated parts of social structure".

During the 1980s and 1990s it was Jon Elster who redeveloped the idea of social mechanisms in sociology (Elster, 1983; 1989). One thing is to point out connections between phenomena. Pointing out satisfactory explanations to these connections is something entirely different. This is what social mechanisms are assigned to do. They represent different causal explanations that we are interested in. This is being discussed in part II of the chapter.

A social mechanism explains what will happen, how it is going to happen and why it happens (Bunge, 1967). Social mechanisms are primarily social constructs, not necessarily capable of being observed, i.e. they are epistemological rather than ontological. On the other hand, however, they are capable of being observed in their social consequences, i.e. we cannot observe the intention, but are able to interpret it in light of social consequences manifested by it through the action. Preferences can also be a social mechanism for economic behaviour. We can not observe people's preferences, but we can interpret them in light of the social consequences they manifest. Social mechanisms are, when understood in this way, analytical constructs, which draw the attention to links between occurrences (Hernes, 1998).

By a social system is here meant a system "composed of people and their artefacts" (Bunge, 1996:21). Social systems are interlinked (in systemic thinking) by dynamic social relations (e.g. emotions, conceptions, norms) and social actions (e.g. cooperation, solidarity, conflict, exchange, communication).

Bunge (1997:414) says: "---a mechanism is a process in a concrete system, such that is capable of being about or preventing some change in the system". It is therefore important to make a distinction between social mechanisms and their consequences,

Social mechanisms operate in concrete systems, e.g. in groups, between groups, in organisations, among organisations, in the ecosystem, etc., and not in conceptual systems or semiotic systems (symbolic systems).

A system is referred to by elements related to one another, and to other systems. A system maintains its identity by means of the relation: the system in its environment. It maintains stability (structure) by means of the total-partial relation, and changes through the reorganisation of relational changes. This can be described figuratively as done in figure 1

Figure 1. Basic social mechanism in concrete systems.

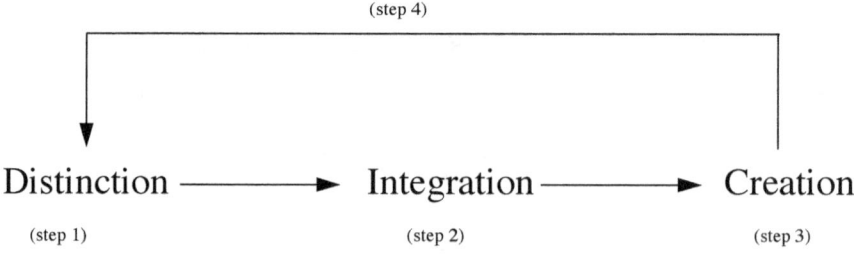

## Social mechanisms

### Step 1: Distinction

When a distinction between the system and other systems in the environment is made, the resulting process is that the identity of the system is established and/or maintained, i.e. the system in the environment relation is established.

### Step 2: Integration

Integration takes place through the development or reinforcement of relations. The resulting process is the establishment of stability, i.e. the total-partial relation.

### Step 3: Creation

Creation is the social mechanism changing the system of relations. The resulting process is social changes in the system, i.e. the reorganisation of relations.

### Step 4: Creativity

As a result of changing the system of relations a distinction process is initiated, where the creatively new, i.e. what has previously not existed, is being established, i.e. innovation is created.

The distinction is the social mechanism initiating and perpetuating the identity process. Integration is the social mechanism initiating and perpetuating the stability process. Creation is the social mechanism initiating and perpetuating the stability process. Creation is the social mechanism initiating and perpetuating change processes, simultaneously with creation along with a new distinction process initiating and perpetuating creativity and innovation processes in social systems.

The three basic mechanisms in social systems are here understood as: Distinction, integration and creation. It is meaningless to speak of social mechanism in conceptual systems, even if the conceptual system will constitute representations of mechanisms expressed by some symbolic system.

A figurative rendering is shown in figure 2

Figure 2. Basic mechanisms and the main processes in social systems

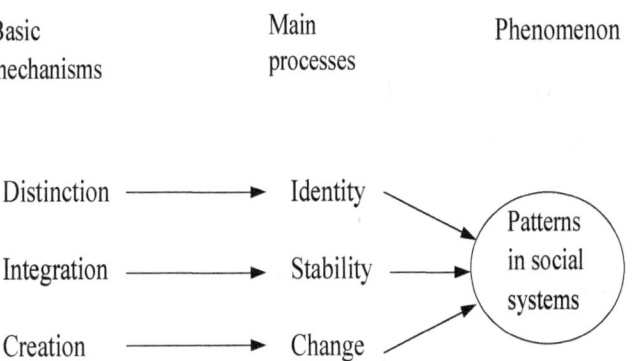

The processes in the social system: Identity, stability and change, are linked to one or more of the partial systems which, according to systemic thinking, constitute a social system. These partial systems are (Bunge, 1996): The economic, the political, the cultural and the social (relationships)

The social mechanisms for the economic partial system are material resources and technology. The social mechanism for the political partial system is power. For the cultural partial system the social mechanisms are expressed through the basic values. The social mechanisms for the social partial system are expressed through human relations. These system-specific social mechanisms interact with each other to achieve certain goals, maintain them, or avoid certain unintended states in the system or the environment.

The system-specific social mechanisms of the individual partial system: Material resources/technology, power, values and human relations, also influence the main processes of social systems, i.e. identity, stability and change.

We will therefore have a hierarchy of social mechanisms in social systems: Basic mechanisms and system-specific mechanisms.

Figuratively this can be expressed as shown in figure 3.

Figure 3  Figurative rendering of social mechanisms

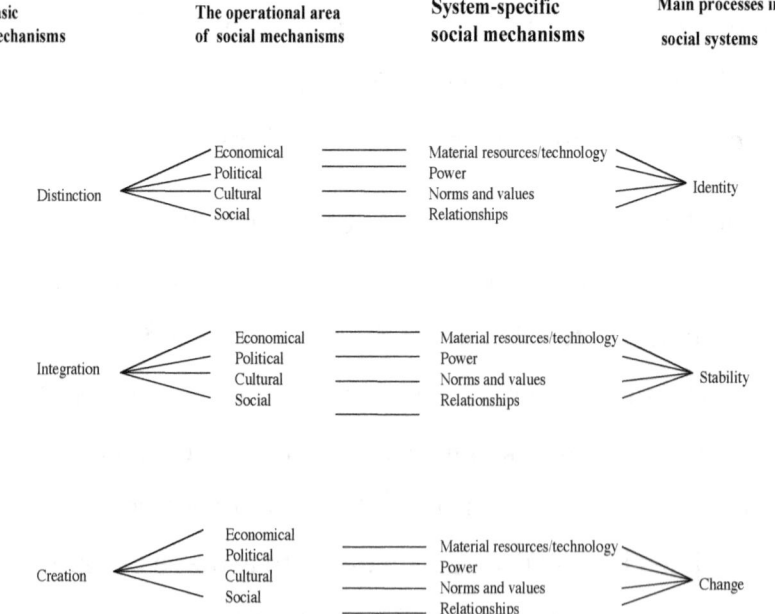

Social mechanisms can be attached to a variety of explanation elements.

The explanation elements can be:

1. Cause-effect oriented, i.e. a linear explanation type
2. Teleological, i.e. an expectation dimensions is linked to the explanation element, i.e. a linear explanation type.
3. Cybernetic, i.e. A has an influence on B, but B has an influence on A, i.e. a circular explanation type.
4. Pattern-disclosing, i.e. a link between the points 1, 2 and 3 above, but where the link results in something **qualitatively** new, and not a summation logic from point 1 to point 3, i.e. that in the pattern-disclosing explanation type there is an emergent entity in relation to the points 1 through 3, i.e. a circular explanation type.

Social mechanisms and explanation models

How can then the knowledge about social mechanisms be used to further explanations of phenomena/problems in social systems?

Explanation means (etymologically) to make what is unknown known. There are certain requirements pertaining to a social mechanism in a scientific context. It must, firstly, be concrete.

This is central, as a mechanism is something operating in the social world (or nature) and not in models of the social world. This is a major distinction, lest we confuse the map with the terrain. Social mechanisms must furthermore be unambiguous, since in the event of ambiguity, the explanation is also going to be ambiguous, thus reducing the explanatory potential of the mechanism. It will then constitute a parallel to any mystical or occult entity capable of changing individuals and social systems if believed in to a sufficient extent. Social mechanisms must, thirdly, be capable of being tested, or any wild speculation will be able to function as a social mechanism.

The critical factor to realise is that a social mechanism is an ontological category, and an explanation is an epistemological category, whereas comprehension is a psychological category (Bunge, 1997:455). I.e. we can understand a phenomenon/problem if we can refer to a social mechanism in the social system, which can explain the phenomenon/problem.

A systemic explanation of how social systems function requires a disclosure of the basic mechanisms (Bunge, 1997:441), i.e. must show how individual mechanisms (micro level) function, and how individual mechanisms are linked (macro level), and possibly how emergent mechanisms appear when more mechanisms vary in relation to each other. It is in other words the link between micro mechanisms and macro-mechanisms which constitutes the most interesting aspect of a systemic approach, in order to explain the mode of function by social systems.

Figuratively this can be seen as in figure 4.

Figure 4. The link between micro and macro mechanisms in social systems.

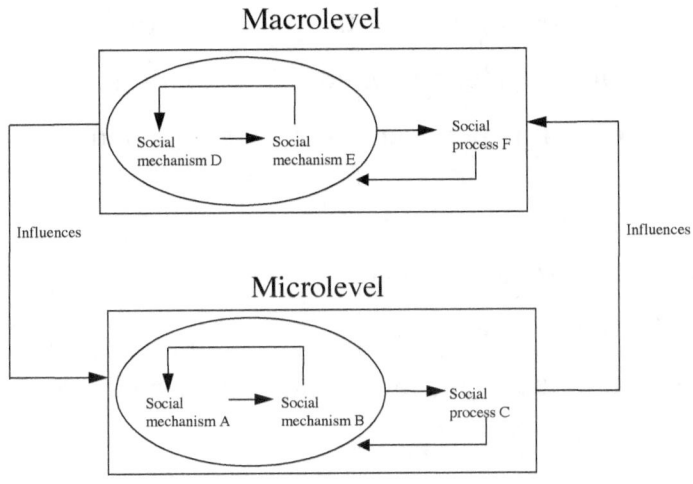

The point of view apparent from figure 4 is that the micro level influences the macro level and that this in turn influences the micro level. Systemic explanations are in this way an alternative to individualistic explanations and holistic explanations (Bunge, 1997:457).

There is a difference between processes in social systems and mechanisms. Social mechanisms keep social processes in progress, but are not the processes. E.g. change processes are a very typical feature of organisations today. One of the social mechanisms acting as the driving force for these change processes (E) is the reorganisation of social relations (RS). That there is a circular link between E and RS does not change this circumstance. That there are also change processes at various levels of social systems (see fig.4), in turn influencing social relations, does not have an impact on the fact that what makes change processes continue, is the reorganisation of social relations. Confusion enters when we do not link macro and micro, and see the link between them. There is then the link between:

1. Social systems at various levels
2. Mechanisms and processes
3. Social systems at various levels and their respective mechanisms and processes.

This means that social mechanisms are part of, but different from processes in progress in social systems. The point is only that by intervening in social mechanisms we can also change the processes, but not vice versa.

The difficulty of disclosing social mechanisms, and separating them for the processes is, among other things, explained by the fact that mechanisms are processes too (Bunge, 1997: 414), and that it is difficult to distinguish the one process from the others in social systems. A social mechanism can, however, be distinguished from other social processes, because mechanisms are developed to reach, maintain or avoid certain targets.

A methodology following from what has been discussed here can be expressed in the following manner:

1.     Investigate the phenomenon/problem in the larger system of which the system in focus is part.
2.     Investigate how the phenomenon/problem is composed, the relations keeping it together, and the relations to the larger system of which the system in focus is part.
3.     Investigate the micro-macro relations.
4.     Look for social mechanisms maintaining, changing or avoiding goal realisation for the processes involved.
4a. Focus on social mechanisms that are concrete, unambiguous and lend themselves to testing.

5.     Look for social mechanisms linked to economic, cultural, political and social partial systems.

6. Explain how social mechanisms influence system behaviour.

## Elaborating on social mechanisms and causal relations in social systems

One important concern in research on social systems, from a systemic point of view, is to reveal patterns, however unimportant they may seem, "and possibly also predict social facts" (Bunge, 1985a:157). This is also emphasised by Glaser & Straus (1967: 3). When revealing patterns, we try to find the phenomena causing variation in the behaviour of systems.

The systemic point of view is that patterns of social behaviour, even if they are all created by individuals or groups, are only rarely a result of momentary considerations. They develop in concert with social groups in the course of time. They are limited by laws of nature, ecological circumstances and tradition, and they are weaker when the group they regulate breaks down, even if they may be incorporated in the culture to the extent that they exist long after they have ceased to have a function.

The ultimate goal in all social science, viewed in a systemic perspective, is to find or uncover patterns conducive to explanations and predications. But most social patterns are local, in the sense that they appear exclusively in societies of a special type. Universal and cross-cultural patterns are however to be found, along with the local ones.

Social scientists can not overlook values, if they are to understand peoples behaviour. And we have to try to understand what values people in various social groups treasure the most. We must further analyse the consistency of the various value patterns, knowing that any value is in conflict with one or more other values. Maintaining the maxim of social science being devoid of values, we will treat people as automates. The solution is not to overlook values, but to study them scientifically.

Some sociologists, as well as economists, try to explain all social facts in terms of the rationality principle. This principle is based on the *hypothesis* that any person, choosing between various action patterns, will choose whatever will maximise his expected utility, i.e. the result where the value (utility) multiplied by the probability of a positive result, is greatest. There are at least three problems in connection with this principle:

1. It requires the liberty on the part of any actor to choose, which is a dubious supposition.

2. Secondly, the value (utility) and the probability involved is subjective, i.e. is difficult to check.

3. Thirdly, the principle is normative, not descriptive. It characterises the rational actor, not the real ones. This means that in reality the principle is irrefutable. Any error in the chosen course of action can be criticised by referring to erroneous observations on the part of the actor with regards to values (utility) and probability.

The rationality principle, interpreted as explained, would perpetuate itself and enclose itself, rendering all criticism impossible, i.e. would tend to be an almost non-scientific principle.

In social research we often encounter the question: What is the cause of X? In social systems causal relationships are more complex and at least different than in the crude physical nature. In the crude physical nature we will often, however not always, find a cause realising an effect. Such connections also exist in social systems. This will here be denoted as historical causal processes. In addition to historical causal processes there are at least three other causal processes forming the basis for the explanation of social systems. We have in figure 5 typologized the four causal processes.

## Fig. 5 Types of causal processes

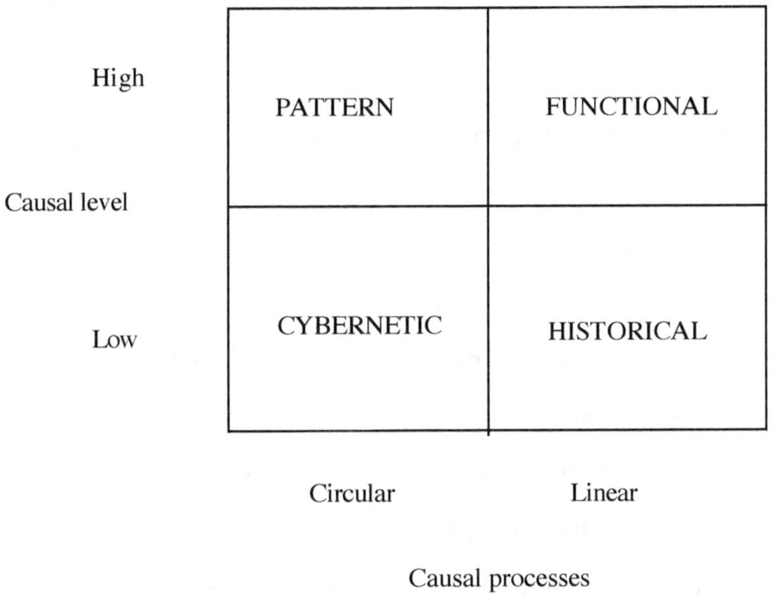

|  | Circular | Linear |
|---|---|---|
| **High** (Causal level) | PATTERN | FUNCTIONAL |
| **Low** | CYBERNETIC | HISTORICAL |

Causal processes

## Historical causal processes and social mechanisms

The causal processes in most frequent use is the historical one (See Hempel, 1965; Salomon, 1989:25-26). This is in figure 5 typologized as a linear causal process at a low causal level. Historical causal processes reflect the existence of an initial cause and a subsequent effect in the direction of time. In the physical world there are many causal flows of this type. In social systems this type of causal context is also evident, but not as pronounced as in physical systems. The following are examples of historical causal processes: conditions of growing up affect behaviour later in life, past events in an organisation affect present behaviour on the part of the employees here and now.

The question linked to historical causal process are of the type: What is the cause of X? E.g. what is the cause of A's behaviour? What we should observe carefully is that this question is also asked when causal processes are not typologized as historical. If the person asking the question is ignorant of the three other types of processes, answers will most certainly be less than illuminating and at worst downright confusing. The knowledge to be derived is that we as researchers must be made aware of what causal processes exist in the social system on which we want to comment before we ask the question, the answer being frequently inherent in the very question.

Functional causal processes and social mechanisms

Questions in connection with functional causal processes are of the type: What does X attempt to accomplish by his acts, behaviour etc.? Functional processes are linked to an expectation mechanism (See Braithwaite, 1953; Wright, 1976; Bigelow & Pargetter, 1987). While cause in historical processes is always linked to the past, expectation is linked to the future. It is for this reason we have typologized the historical and functional processes as linear. There is either a "line" from the past to a present situation (historical causal connections), or a "line" from the future (expectation) to the present situation (functional causal connections). In literature functional causal connections are denoted as teleological, since they are linked to future goals for the person or the system (See Radcliffe-Brown, 1952; Malinowski, 1954; Merton, 1957; Nagel, 1977). Examples of functional connections are: To look for someone's motive is potentially of a functional type. What motive relative to his action did Per have? But here we should realise that the motive can also be linked to an historical event, i.e. an historical social mechanisms is in operation, not an expectation mechanism. If we not clarify which causal connection is in operation, explanation appearing at a subsequent level might be misleading. A more obvious example of a functional context, is questions related to future goals on the part of the system. E.g.: What is the professors goal regarding student guidance? What goals is the company trying to reach? What is Knut's object of drinking? Take a closer look at the last question? The reply or the replies would provide a completely different type of insight than if it had been: What is the cause of Knut drinking? The latter question brings to mind a historical causal connection and limits solution proposals to involve search for events in the past which could prove helpful in future treatment. The first question, on the other hand, brings to mind an expectation mechanism, and a potential treatment will then be different from what it would have been, had if the second question had not been asked. That both causal connections should be used in relation to the problem in question and other problems, is today seen as a foregone conclusion. But in other areas that is not necessarily the case.

## Cybernetic causal processes and social mechanisms

Circular causal models are relatively new in a research context and can be traced back to the 1940s. Cybernetics in figure 5 is linked to feedback processes (See Rosenblueth, Wiener & Bigelow, 1943). Some examples would explain this. People raise their children, but children also raise their parents. The working environment affects productivity, but productivity also affects the working environment. Teachers influence their students, but students also influence their teachers. Advertising influences consumers, but consumers also influence the lay-out of advertising. The leader influences the employees, but the employees also influence the behaviour of the leader. Aggressive behaviour leads to deprecatory attitudes, enforcing aggressive behaviour. The means affect the end, but the end also affects the means etc.

The question linked to cybernetic processes is of the following type: What sustains an act, behaviour etc..? The answer, at a general level, is that it is the feed-back mechanism which sustains the act, behaviour etc. At a concrete and practical level it is important to find out what this feed-back mechanism consists of. Its existence in social systems is a universally acknowledged fact (See Ashby, 1961; 1970; 1981). What the researcher must do is to reveal the identity of the critical feed-back mechanisms in systems and situations which we want to make comments on.

Circular processes are characterised by feedback loops. We can distinguish between two main types of feed-back. It is the ones which have been developed to head towards a prearranged goal (negative feedback) (See Nagel, 1956 1961),and those which appear to inflate themselves, according to an accumulative principle (positive feedback) (See Maruyama, 1963). A positive feedback mechanism has a tendency to destabilize social systems. The researcher must therefore disclose to what extent it is negative or positive feedback which dominates the social system subject to study.

If we view the system on the basis of circular understanding, it is futile to look for one or more causes. It is how critical entities interact which becomes the interesting field of study, in order to explain the causal processes. If we in the study of a social system extracts one or more entities and denote them as cause, the entire explanation of system behaviour will take on a new meaning, compared to what it would if based on circular processes.

## Pattern processes and social mechanisms

Patterns is the most complex of the four explanation types we have typologized in figure 5. Patterns can not be quantified for the simple reason that patterns are neither numbers, nor quantities, but are of a different and more elevated logical type than both number and quantity (See Bateson, 1972;1979). The case of mistaken identity which often occurs, is due to the fact that number and quantity form the basis for patterns, but they are not patterns. It is the disclosure of patterns which is interesting in this process, both because pattern disclosure precedes the development of social laws, but also because pattern disclosure reveals something about how the components and the complete structure of social systems relate to one another (See Hanson, 1958). The question linked to this type of causal processes is: What is the pattern of which e.g. system behaviour is part? A pattern is linked both to an historical causal process, to feed-back mechanisms, in addition to expectation mechanisms. One example might provide conducive to the understanding of patterns. If person A has a relationship to person B, a change in expectations which e.g. person B has regarding his future position, career etc., might cause person A to change his behaviour toward B instantly. Another example is the communication pattern of a family. If a family conflict is headed towards an emotional breaking point, the emergence of a specific pattern according to which communication will adhere, will be evident fairly soon. Firstly the instant feedback mechanisms will be in operation, i.e. the particular behaviour (smiling, shake of head, clearing one's throat etc.) could easily reinforce a negative pattern, in the same way as taciturnity might generate explosive behaviour. Secondly, expectations of a future happening, not necessarily related to the conflict in question, might be introduced as an argument in the conflict. Thirdly historical events, possibly dating a long time back, might easily be brought into the conflict, despite their lack of relevancy to the situation at hand. The result is that with a great degree of certainty, a positive feedback mechanism will be in operation, and the conflict will get out of control, with the subsequent well-known solution mechanisms. If we, in the imagined capacity of family researcher, ask the question: What is the cause of this conflict getting out of control?, the answers are likely to display a certain inclination towards historical causal explanations, whereas entirely different mechanisms were really the ones in operation.

Pattern is the synthesis of the three other causal connections. But this is also crucial for the understanding of patterns, the synthesis possibly being different from the sum of the other three causal connections. Sometimes the synthesis can be more than the sum of the other three causal contexts. On other occasions the synthesis may be less than the sum of the other three causal connections. On some rare occasions the synthesis can equal the sum of the three other causal contexts. Patterns are, on the basis of the above discussion, a causal process qualitatively different from the other three.

The four causal processes are not reciprocally preclusive, but have to be regarded as complementary if we are to understand and explain social mechanisms in social systems. All types should be used in the study of social systems, but preferably questions adequate to each of them. Only in this way will our explanations be sufficient.

## Elaborating on social mechanisms and pattern processes

We will typologize four pattern processes in this part. They are: empirical generalisations, models, theories and social laws.

Empirical generalisations constitute a type of patterns in social systems. These are summing up data or making generalisations on the basis of data (See Rescher, 1962). An empirical generalisation is only substituted by the data from which it emerged, and is usually lacking in terms of a theory explaining these connections. If new data, which does not support these empirical generalisation materialise, it will have to be discarded, due to the fact that there is nothing to fall back on (See Hempel, 1962; 1962a; 1965; 1968).

Models being used in a research context, can be understood as a type of pattern of a social system. The models explain something about the connection between variables in the social system. The models are, as opposed to empirical generalisations and social laws, not confirmed through confrontation with data, being conceptually determined by one or more observers, and can be regarded as a help for the researcher in his attempts to disclose a pattern.

Social laws constitute patterns of a unique type: they are

systemic, i.e. linked to a knowledge system, and are not changed unless facts which they represent change (See Bunge, 1983; 1983a). The essential difference between a law statement and other statements are:

1. Law statement are general,

2. They are systemic, i.e. linked to an existing knowledge system, and

3. They have been confirmed through many studies.

A pattern can be seen as stable variables over a certain period of time. A social law is created by an observer who gets insight into this pattern. By acquiring insight into patterns of social behaviour, we are also in the position to predict parts of this behaviour, at least make a rough estimate and in a shorter time perspective.

Social laws are further linked to special societies in time and space, but the linking to time and space can also to a great extent be applied to laws of nature, despite their longer time perspective and more general nature compared to social laws.

Theories are also a type of patterns, namely patterns of relations between propositions (See Hempel, 1962; Bunge, 1985; 1985 a). Theories can be useful for making specific predictions (See Gardner, 1979) and can increase our information processing capability. Figure 6 typologies social patterns previously discussed.

Fig. 6 Various types of social patterns

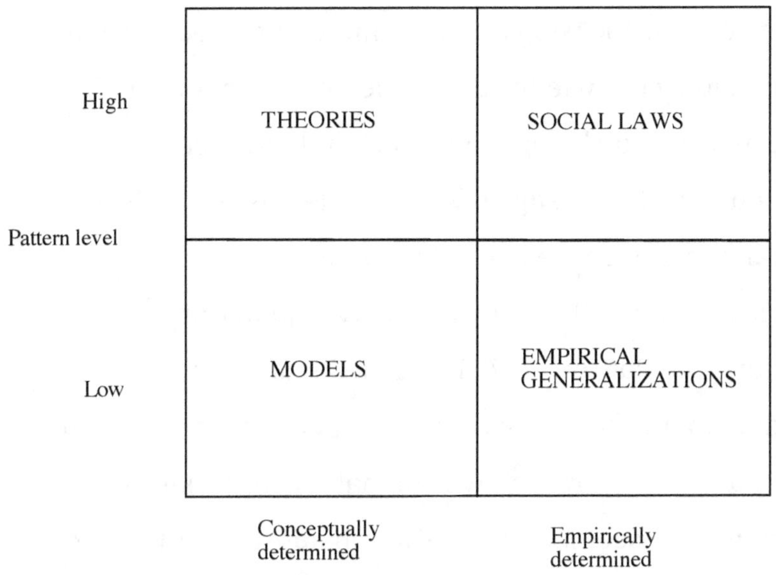

|  | Conceptually determined | Empirically determined |
|---|---|---|
| **High** Pattern level | THEORIES | SOCIAL LAWS |
| **Low** | MODELS | EMPIRICAL GENERALIZATIONS |

Models and empirical generalizations are typologized at a low pattern level, as they contain descriptive knowledge. Theories and social laws are typologized at a high pattern level, as they contain explanatory elements. By means of the explanatory elements it would be possible to make statements about some of the necessary and sufficient conditions for system change. It is the underlying mechanisms, the entities which cannot be unobserved which constitutes the information in explanatory knowledge in relation to descriptive knowledge. Explanatory knowledge is complementary and precedes the actual predication. E. g. when we have the explanation of why birds gather at a specific point in the Bird Island Fjord, we may safely conclude that there is fish in the area. The fish below the ocean surface is not visible to the naked eye, but we can have knowledge of it by focusing upon the indicators, because we have explanatory knowledge about the phenomenon. In this way we can distinguish between direct and indirect observation. Our knowledge of observables relies on the theoretical knowledge we have of the phenomenon. Our knowledge at hand will usually be partly explanatory information (See Railton, 1978), not the ideal accurate information about the whole range of aspects which bring the phenomenon about. The partly explanatory information is central to the law-seeking pragmatic consideration of the phenomenon.

The distinction between explanation and predication is a pragmatic one. i.e. the predication is meant as the practical relevancy requirement in a research process, which is then to be tested by e.g. the practitioners. Predication is meant to ensure the practical adequate application of the research. Explanatory knowledge attempts to disclose the operational processes in system behaviour, so that the black box becomes grey or even nearly white.

## Social mechanisms, models and theories

We act on the basis of cognitive models. If our models of reality are erroneous, our acts will also have consequences which could be harmful for the surroundings.

The fact that our model of a social phenomenon/problem will be different to each and every one of us, can be explained by means of the three underlying mechanisms (See Bandler & Grinder, 1975).

1. We generalise on the basis of the social sphere.

2. We select something and discard something else.

3. We make distortions and changes of which we are not conscious.

When making statements describing the social world, it is basically our own models of the social reality which we express ourselves about. This is completely different from contending that it is the so-called objective social reality we express ourselves about.

The process in operation when making our models of a social phenomenon/problem, is also in operation when communicating to others how a phenomenon or problem is.

The underlying mechanisms can be expressed in the following manner (See Bandler & Grinder, 1975):

A. We make generalization's on the basis of our experiences.

B. We by-and-large make selective picks from our memory, and

C. We distort, or are creative in relation to what we select from our memory, making it distorted in relation to what we have stored originally.

Abstract phenomena are of prime importance when building models. But the usefulness of abstract phenomena can only be demonstrated when confronted with a specific empirical problem.

In order to understand a phenomenon, visualising how the variation in a variable is related to the variation in another variable is a requirement. If the concepts are to be useful in a model context, they have to be attached to each other. Such connections between concepts then form theoretical propositions. These statements specify the way in which the phenomenon is structured. E.g. the more persons with higher competence than ourselves we are in touch with, the higher the probability of developing new ideas. When propositions about a specific phenomenon is integrated into a system, a theory will have been developed by us. The theory can be small and limited, it can cover a medium-sized area, or it can cover a large area of social reality.

There are two types of models which can be helpful in our efforts to make comments on a specific phenomenon. These models will here be referred to as analytical (Turner, 1991) and causal. It is really two types of causal models we use. Firstly, it is conceptually causal models, where the relations between concepts conducive to operationalization are in focus. Secondly, it is empirical-causal models. Here a conceptually causal model is used in an empirical investigation, and we elicit statistical correlation's between concepts in the conceptually causal model.

The more dissociated the concepts in a model are from reference to specific empirical cases, the higher is the level of abstraction or the degree of reach on the part of the model. The more investigations are covered by the concepts and the theoretical statements in an approach, the greater is the range of the model.

## Fig. 7 Various approaches to research problems

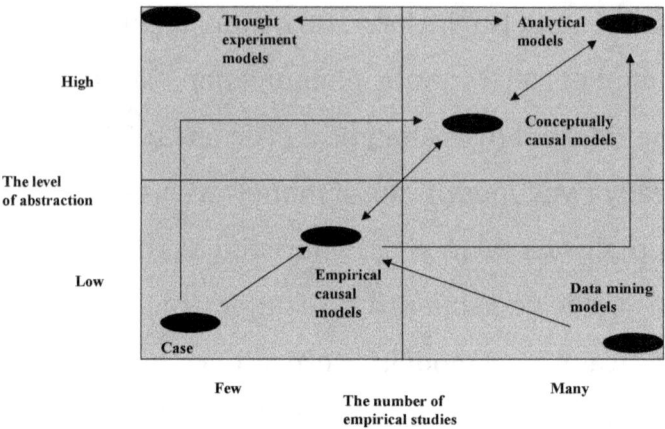

The indicators in figure 7 show the connection between the various approaches. E.g. we can use case studies to develop conceptually causal models, and empirical causal models. Conceptually causal models and empirical causal models can both be helpful in the development of analytical models, as can thought experiment models be. But analytical models can also form the basis for the development of conceptually causal models.

Causal models are tied to specific empirical contexts. An empirical causal model usually involves correlation statements and couples empirically measured variables. Before we can depict the empirical connections in a model, we will develop a conceptually causal model, which will be used in a specific study. This model may either be developed from an analytical model, or case studies, or both. When the conceptual causal model is developed, we will design a survey on the basis of the model, and conduct the empirical study. The results of the study will then appear in the form of an empirical causal model, which also can be a result of data-mining models. The empirical causal model will now involve correlation statements between variables. E.g. education and idea generation correlate with 0.67. The empirical causal model can be used to support or change contexts in the analytical and conceptual causal model. In this way knowledge is accumulated in the analytical model, and we will gradually be in a better position to see contexts and patterns in the phenomenon about which we want to make comments. The analytical model can form the basis for the development of small theories about a specific phenomenon, and also generate social laws, i.e. social mechanisms will awaken from their sarcophagi and generate social laws in social science.

Analytical models have great insight, but are difficult to test in their full context. They contain a lot of abstract concepts, and their connections are too diverse to be tested directly (see Turner, 1988;1991). To what extent are then analytical models conducive to the accumulation of knowledge? The forte of these models is to specify how processes and social mechanisms, in which the concepts are included, are coupled.

Analytical models can also be useful as a starting point for theory building. By isolating basic processes and social mechanisms and showing their connection structure, we may develop a notion of the most important social processes and social mechanisms in the phenomenon subject to study, or part of it. They can also be helpful in developing hypotheses later to be tested in causal models. Even if the analytical models can not be tested in their full context, due to their complexity, we can decompose causal models and hypotheses from these, which can in turn be tested empirically. The most essential connection when accumulating knowledge about a phenomenon, is the one between analytical models, causal models and hypotheses, says Turner (1991). There is a creative synergy in play in the shift between the translation of analytical models to causal models and formal hypotheses. When empirical tests have been conducted we can later return to the analytical models and possibly make corrections.

The analytical model functions as a large-scale survey chart. It is to be regarded as a bird's eye view of the phenomenon/problem subject to study. In the bird's eye view we should all realise that: Firstly, one perspective is conveyed, precluding all others. The preclusion of others, does not preclude the possibility of other perspectives being every bit as interesting in terms of explaining the phenomenon/problem. This only means that we have chosen to focus on elements that other perspectives might open up.

Secondly, details in the bird's eyes view have a tendency to get blurry. Details, on the other hand, are more apparent in the conceptually causal model. This model can be viewed as a survey chart, displaying more diversity in the terrain then the bird's eye view would.

By means of the analytical model, we attempt to explain what critical variables will be critical for a specific phenomenon. What the empirical tests are to inform us about, is what entities will in all likelihood generate e.g. increased innovation capacity on the part of companies. Some entities will always be more crucial than others. The greater the connections between the entities in the model, the greater the degree of certainty in our recommendations of change in the system to the principal.

The individual models can be developed through case studies, literature examination, analogies to similar phenomena, and deduction from theory. Tests are empirical studies aimed at supporting and possibly changing the original models, so that, as they gradually comprise an increasingly wider material, will be more robust and reliable. The ultimate goal of this procedure will be pragmatic, i.e. the degree of certainty with which recommendations can be given e.g. to activities according to the pattern: If you want X, do y, x etc. In other words, it is the practical application of the models which constitutes the goal of the strategy.

Through testing, model change, new testing etc., we will acquire knowledge leading up to increased insight on the part of analytical and conceptual causal models. In this way it is possible to systematise knowledge, and gradually get in a position to gain insight into entities which are detrimental/conducive to e.g. innovation in companies.

In order to test the conceptually causal model, the concepts must be operationalized, making them suitable to use in a survey and/or more case studies.

The model is a description of entities that can be observed. In order to explain why things are the way the model describes, we must operate at a more basic level, where entities incapable of being observed exist. For this purpose theory is necessary.

A theory poses supposed explanations to a phenomenon by means of entities which we for the most part can not observe. A model, on the other hand, refers to entities capable of being observed and compared. It would have been intellectually stimulating to have a theory for e.g. innovation. But a model which turns out to function in practice, is adequate for a practical purpose.

## Conclusion

What knowledge do we have when explaining e.g. innovation in companies by means of a theory which we would not have by means of a functional model? The answer is really simple. We can then make statements about the underlying causal processes and social mechanisms on which the model is based. If there is no existing theory on the phenomenon we are trying to say something about, we can develop models disclosing partial knowledge regarding this phenomenon. This is the case with a lot of phenomena in the social world, ie. we can find social mechanisms which explains what will happen, when and why.

A theory will constitute a continuous system of statements explaining causal processes and social mechanisms in function relative to the phenomenon. One or more procedures to obtain greater insight into the phenomenon, is a reciprocal action between case, causal models, causal empirical models and analytical models. But however well-functioning models we develop, we will by means of this procedure not have developed a theory of the phenomenon. For that purpose explanations at a more basic level than what the model are able to disclose, will be necessary.

The empirical causal model says something about the strength in the relation between the variables and can be used in practice in order to change certain variables to facilitate the desired change in the system.

The relationship between a model and a theory is equivalent to the relationship between descriptive knowledge and explanatory knowledge. But before we reach the point where we can explain a phenomenon, we must be able to describe what happens. I.e. we must be informed regarding certain social mechanisms pertaining to the phenomenon. We can e.g. say that there is a correlation between education and the generation of creative ideas. But we will still be unable to give a convincing explanation as to the appearance of this correlation. An explanation will often, however not always, bring about other phenomena which are not subject to direct observation. It is there, behind the factors which can be observed and compared, a theory will take us.

If possible, explanations at a more basic level would be desirable. But it is not necessary for the application of insights in practical contexts. By this we have stated that a theory can be desirable, but not necessary, in order to develop e.g. innovative organisations. Models and social mechanisms, on the other hand, are necessary to organise knowledge for the purpose of use in practical contexts.

# References

Ashby, W.R. 1961. An Introduction to Cybernetics. New York: Chapman & Hall LTD.

Ashby, W.R. 1970. Connectance of Large Dynamic (Cybernetic) Systems: Critical Values for Stability. Nature, Vol 228 no. 5273 Nov. 21.

Ashby, W.R. 1981. What is an Intelligent Machine? In Conant, R. (Ed.), Mechanisms of Intelligence. California: Intersystems Seaside.

Bandler, R. & Grinder, J. 1975. The Structure of Magia. Vol I & Vol II. Palo Alto, Cal: Science and Behavior Books.

Bateson, G. 1972. Steps to a Ecology of Mind. London: Intex Books.

Bateson, G. 1979. Mind and Nature. (Swedish Translation, 1988, Stockholm:Symposium & Tryckeri ).

Bigelow, J. and Pargetter, R. 1987. Functions, Journal of Philosophy, 84: 181-196.

Braithwaite, R.B. 1953. Scientific Explanation. Cambridge: Cambridge University Press.

Bunge, M. (1967). Scientific Research, Vol. 3, in studies of the foundations methodology and philosophy of science, Springer Verlag, Berlin.

Bunge, M. 1983. Exploring the World. Dordrecht: Reidel.

Bunge, M. 1983a. Understanding the World. Dordrecht: Reidel.

Bunge, M. 1985. Philosophy of Science and Technology. Part I. Dordrecht: Reidel.

Bunge, M. 1985a. Philosophy of Science and Technology. Part II. Dordrecht: Reidel.

Bunge, M.1996. Finding Philosophy in Social Science.

New Haven CT: Yale University Press.

Bunge, M.1997. Mechanism and explanation. Philosophy of the Social Sciences 27: 410-465.

Bunge, M..1998. Social Science under Debate. Toronto: University of Toronto Press.

Bunge,M..1999. The Sociology-Philosophy Connection. New Brunswick NJ: Transaction Publishers.

Elster, J. (1983). Explaining technical change: A case study in the philosophy of science, Cambridge University Press, Cambridge.

Elster, J. 1989. Nuts and bolts for the social sciences, Cambridge University Press, Cambridge.

Gardner, M. 1979. Realism and instrumentalism in the 19th Century, Philosophy of Science, 46: 645-650.

Glaser, B.G. & Strauss, A.L. 1967. The Discovery of Grounded Theory: Strategies for qualitative research. New York: Aldine De Gruyter.

Hanson, N.R.1958. Patterns of Discovery. Cambridge: Cambridge University Press.

Hempel, C.G.1962. Deductive-Nomological vs. Statistical Explanations. In Feigl, H. & Maxwell, G. (eds.), Minesota Studies in the Philosophy of Science. Vol III. Minneapolis: University of Minesota Press.

Hempel, C.G.1962a. Explanations in Science and in History. In Colodny, R.G. (Ed.), Frontiers of Science and Philosophy: 7-34, Pittsburgh:University of Pittsburgh Press.

Hempel, C.G.1965. Aspects of Scientific Explanation. New York: Free Press.

Hempel, C.G.1968. Maximal Specificity and Lawlikeness in Probabilistic Explanations, Philosophy of Science, 35: 116-133.

Hernes, G. (1998). Real virtuality, in social mechanisms: An analytical approach to social theory, edited by Peter Hedstrøm and Richard Swedberg, Cambridge University Press, Cambridge (pp. 74-102)

Malinowski, B. 1954. Magic, Science and Religion, and other Essays. Garden City: Doubleday Anchor Books.

Maruyama, M. 1963. The Second Cybernetics: Deviation Amplifying Mutual Causal Processes, American Scientist, 51: 164-179.

Merton, R.K. 1957. Social Theory and Social Structure. New York, Free Press.

Merton, R.K. (1967). On sociological theory of the middle range, in On theoretical sociology, Free Press, New York (pp. 39-72)

Merton, R.K. (1968). Social theory and social structure, Free Press, New York.

Nagel, E. 1956. A Formalization of Functionalism. In Nagel, E. (Ed.), Logic Without Metaphysics: 247-283. Glencoe: Free Press.

Nagel, E. 1961. The Structure of Science: Problems in the Logic of Scientific Explanation. New York: Harcourt, Brace & World.

Nagel, E. 1977. Teleology Revisited, Journal of Philosophy, 74: 261-301.

Radcliffe-Brown, A.R. 1952. Structure and Function in Primitive Society. London: Cohen and West Ltd.

Railton, P. 1978. A Deductive-Nomological Model of Probabilistic Explanation, Philosophy of Science, 45: 206-226.

Rescher, N. 1962. The Stochastic Revolution and the Nature of Scientific Explanation, Synthese, 14: 200-215.

Rosenblueth, A., Wiener, N. & Bigelow, J. 1943. Behavior, Purpose and Teleology, Philosophy of Science, 10: 18-24.

Salmon, W.C. 1989. Four Decades of Scientific Explanation. In Kitcher, P. and Salmon, W.C. (eds.), Scientific Explanation: Minnesota Studies in the Philosophy of Science: 3-220. Vol. XIII. Minneapolis: University of Minnesota Press.

Turner, J. 1988. A Theory of Social Interaction. Stanford, Cal.: Polity Press.

Turner, J. 1991. The Structure of Sociological Theory. Belmont, Cal.: Wadsworth Publishing Company.

Wright, L. 1976. Teleological Explanations. London:University of California Press.

# Part III Explaining change

## Chapter 3 Institutional changes

Introduction

The institutional legitimacy has, according to Scott (1995:37), two forms, cognitive legitimacy and normative legitimacy. Cognitive legitimacy is concerned about what we take for granted, and how this has possibly been changed. Statements of the type: this is how we do it around here, represents this cognitive authority. This expresses common conceptions or common mental models, which determines the thought pattern in a total activity. To what extent an activity is cognitively closed to the outside world or more cognitively open to the outside world, says something about the ability to learn on the part of the activity. Normative legitimacy is engrained in the social pressure brought to bear directly or indirectly on its actors. It is here relevant to speak of normative openness or closedness. The more normatively closed a system is, the more self-referential the system becomes, and the less comparison with other systems in the environment takes place.

Institutional factors, cognitive and normative legitimacy, can be focused around cognitive closeness/openness and normative closeness/openness.

The cognitive part can be regarded as a thought pattern and the normative part as an action pattern. Seen in this way, it is our thought and action pattern which opens versus closes institutions. This perspective gives us access to understanding and explanation of changes in institutions.

The question to be focused on in this chapter is: How can we explain institutional changes? There are changes in institutions that are difficult to explain. To understand is a psychological mode, while explaining is a methodological mode. To understand is linked to involvement and absorption, while explanation is linked to the understanding of stability and change at the system level by means of historical links, e.g. the changes in relative prices due to technological changes. Stability and change at the system level can be explained by means of expectations or as pattern of expectations, e.g. the discontent due to increasing expectations. Stability and change at the individual level can be explained by means of action patterns, e.g. norms and values, ideology, cooperation versus competition.

## Explaining institutional change

The new institutional theory has two developmental features. One is from neo-classical economic thinking. The other school is the Austrian school, in particular Hayek (see Langlois, 1989:291 – 294). The concept of new institutional economy, also called the new theory about organizations, was first used about Williamson (1975). After that important names in this perspective are: Coase, North, Furubotn, Richter etc. Both Ludvik von Mises and Fredrick Hayek, both part of the Austrian school, provided basic points of view regarding the impact of institutions on performance.

In the new institutional economy the individual is in focus. It is the objective, taste, ideas, purpose, behaviour, etc, of the individual, which constitutes the basis for the new institutional economy, and as an explanatory factor for performance in social systems.

This point of view is in complete accordance with the main features of the Austrian school. Inherent in the extension of a new economy is that all systems seek to maximise their own benefit within the framework they operate in. It is further assumed that preferences on the part of individuals change over a period of time (North, 1990). A consequence of changing preferences is that expectations and mental models to be used for the purpose of self-orientation also change. Individuals are expected not to be perfect as rational actors, even if they may have intentions of being rational.

Information and communication costs (info-structure costs) will be too massive for necessary knowledge about a complex phenomenon/problem to be acquired. Therefore the behaviour of the individual is surrounded by ambiguity. Ambiguity can be reduced by means of information, but can be clarified by means of communication. Therefore info-structure costs will be a determining factor for interaction among people.

In a new institutional economy proprietary rights are assumed to have a major impact on performance in social systems. In the extension of proprietary rights contracts play a major part (see Coleman, 1991). The political framework has a direct impact on the development of proprietary rights and the conflict system balancing the latter in the social room. The political framework also has an impact on the development of laws, rules and their interpretation, in addition to systems for the enforcement of laws and regulations.

The new institutional economy is concerned about the rules of the game (institutions and the individuals controlled by these formal and informal rules (see Furubotn & Richter, 1998:7). This means that there are not just historical links and the political framework which determines performance in social systems seen form a new institutional perspective, but also the organisation of stability and change in social systems.

Institutional theory, as opposed to e.g. contingency theory, resource-based theory and transaction cost theory contribute to emphasising the cultural factor in order to understand and explain activities. Institutions can be defined as: "formal and informal rules that constrain individual behaviour and shape human interaction" (Eggerston, 1996:). Informal rules can be constituted by laws, contracts, deals, etc.

## Explaining institutional change: A historical perspective

As shown in part I the historical perspective emphasize linear causal relations.

Institutional analyses also have the focus on how institutions influence performance. I we study performance and changes in systems from an institutional perspective, the historical context is decisive, because historical links influence the organisation and thus performance. It is this very interaction between institutions and organisation that will influence performance and changes in social systems as noted by North (1996:345). Institutions are constituted by formal and informal rules. Formal rules can e.g. be the laws and regulatory mechanisms. Informal rules can e.g. be norms and values in a social system.

Historical links can be used to understand change processes in the economic partial system. The economic partial system does not operate in a vacuum. Its historical bindings can therefore be used to understand relations between the various partial systems constituting the fabric of a social system, i.e. economic, social, cultural, and political partial systems. This type of context has been shown by North (1968), who points out that when relative prices are changed, this is an indication of technological changes.

One of Joseph Schumpeter's argument was that economic history was the most important basis for economic understanding (see Fogel, 1997). One insight into economic history is that institutional factors impact the diffusion of technology (North, 1994). Kuznets (1966) further contends that a change in norms and values promotes mobility and thus influences economic processes. The culture or basic ideology of a society has a tremendous impact on how quickly and efficiently new technology is put to use (see North, 1990). North's historical "law" can be expressed as institutions influencing performance. This "law" can be used in many contexts to explain various performances between different systems. This does not mean that social systems are historically determined, but that the links of history set limits for the performance of social systems.

The most typical historical links are technological and institutional (see Arthur, 1989). Systems and individuals are literally locked in and stigmatised by historical events, for better or worse. There are various conceptions regarding the importance of technological versus institutional attachments in regard to change, stability, and performance. North (1981; 1990), North & Davis (1971) and North& Thomas (1973) emphasise the importance of institutions. Institutions and technology both influence transaction costs and transformation costs, which in turn influence the performance of the system. In order to create change, then one can change each of the abovementioned elements, i.e. institutions, technology, transaction costs, transformation costs and performance.

Even if stability is a necessary condition for complex human interaction (North, 1990:84), then change is a necessary condition for stability (Bateson, 1972). From an economic perspective change in relative prices is the most important social mechanisms for change everywhere (see North, 1981: North & Thomas, 1973). The action rule to be extracted from this intention is the following one: In order for changes in social systems to be uncovered, changes in relative prices should be looked for. E.g. relative prices of: land and work, work and technology, work and capital, technology and competence, competence and creativity, innovation and geographical location.

Changes in relative prices influence the political development, cultural development and as well as changes in the interaction system. In addition to individual actors, innovators and entrepreneurs, etc., will be strongly influenced by changes in relative prices.

Historical links are often reinforced as a result of the success or penetration of e.g. technology influencing a system. When technology is used continuous improvements of the technology are developed, serving to link the individual more strongly to this very type of technology. The inherent force of habit attaches the technology to the user, even if other technologies could generate higher performance. Habits, learning and the use of technology in other systems cause it to have an uncontested position in relation to other competing technologies.

## Explaining institutional change: A cybernetic perspective

As shown in part I the cybernetic perspective emphasize feedback processes. We will ewplain institutional change by this perspective with the focus upon the two constructs: transaction costs and transformation costs.

Transaction costs are here understood as: "the costs of measuring agreements" (North, 1997:9). Williamson (1996:8) says that the transaction perspective is: "the combination of rational spirit, with a system perspective".

Transformation costs can be linked to costs relative to matter/energy in and between systems (see Miller, 1978). Transaction costs can be linked to information functions with Miller (1978). The assumptions behind transaction and transformation costs are limited rationality, i.e.: "intended rational, but limited so (Simon, 1961) and opportunism (see Williamson, 1996:10).

Transaction costs appear in connection with exchange of information, or information linked to the exchange process. The size of and the distribution of these costs influences the organisation of economic activities, among other things. It is not only institutions that will influence transaction costs, but also the technology surrounding the system. A transaction: "occurs when a good or service is transferred across technologically separable interface" (Williamson, 1985:1). Where an activity is completed and a new starts a transaction thus takes place. This definition does not distinguish between transformation costs and transaction costs. The distinction has however been made by us, since in our opinion it creates more analytical understanding and depth of explanation in the transition from the industrial economy logic to the knowledge economy logic, and can help us explain institutional changes. For analytical reasons we will therefore distinguish between transaction costs and transformation costs in the following way: A transaction takes place when information is passed on from one information process to another information process in, or between systems, in such a way that an activity is completed and a new one starts. This transaction incurs an expense for social systems, referred to as transaction cost.

 This understanding is a slight extension of Williamson's transaction theory, which makes it analytically easier to understand and explain the development of organisations and institutions in the knowledge economy. We find support for this interpretation with Miller & Vollman (1985), among others.

Already Adam Smith in his pin example (1776) treated transactions and transformations. Adam Smith points out that it takes X number of transaction and transformations in order to complete the entire process of manufacturing a pin. In Adam Smith's example there is great similarity between transactions, transformations and the division of work internally in the company. Both transactions and transformations can be economic, political, social and cultural. Economic transactions and transformations make up just a small part of actions in social systems. In the new institutional economy it is political and economic transactions as well as transformations which are focused on. Social and cultural transactions are not so usual, but even more important viewed from a performance perspective, or a institutional change perspective.

Transaction and transformation costs can be linked to the establishment, maintenance, and change of economic, political, social and cultural activities in social systems.

Various types of transaction and transformations within the economic area are costs linked to the establishment, maintenance and change of economic operations internally in systems and between the system and the environment, e.g. expectation, incentives and market transactions.

Various types of transactions and transformations within the political field are costs linked to the establishment, maintenance and change of power internally in systems or between the system and the environment, e.g. mental models, ideology, proprietary rights and judical system.

Various types of transactions and transformations within the social field are costs linked to establishing, maintaining and changing social relations internally in systems and between the system and the environment, e.g. creativity, competence and innovation.

Various types of transactions and transformations within the cultural field are costs linked to establishing, maintaining and changing values and norms internally in systems and between the system and the environment, e.g. behaviour and values.

For Coase the starting point for transaction cost thinking was to what extent operations should be self-sufficient in terms of functions or buy functions from the market (see Coase, 1988: 19). In this way boundaries for operations in the business could be stipulated in the following way: When transaction costs linked to carrying out operations yourself exceeds the costs of buying operations form the market, then operations should be outsourced.

In the political partial system resistance and opportunistic behaviour may ensue when transaction costs and transformation costs are changed. In the cultural partial system creative tension is released during changes in transactions and transformation costs.

In social partial systems, relational strain will be released in the event of changes in transaction costs or transformation costs. In the economic system a conflict may easily ensue when transaction and transformation costs are changed. Transaction costs and transformation costs in this way influence the organizing of social systems.

The negative social consequences of organizing, leads to what can be described as organizing costs. Transaction and transformation costs then influence both performance and organizing (see Kreps, 1990).

## Explaining institutional change: A functional perspective

As shown in part I the functional perspective emphasize expectation mechanisms.

Institutions in this way will limit people's interactions, and structure their relations and thus a lot of the communication (see North, 1996:344). Both formal and informal rules exist due to their being accepted as a totality of the social system in which it operates. Both formal and informal rules are maintained by means of cognitive normative expectations. Cognitive expectations are not costly to change in psychological terms. They are less value-oriented. Normative expectations on the other hand are value-oriented, they are taken into consideration and influence behaviour at an unexpressed level. This is the realm of concealed influences, but with major social consequences if observed. Institutions stipulate limitations for the realms of possibility in the interaction between people. In this way institutions influence the possibilities for change and the performance of systems. If the possibility realm is changed, e.g. by changing the possibilities for relations between people, systems will change as a result of relations changing.

While institutions can be understood as the rules of the game, organisations can be seen as a relations between the players (see North, 1997:9). An institution can also be understood as any thought and action system, formally or informally, as framing interactions between people (see North, 1990:4).

Thought and action structures framing the interaction among people are linked to common norms and values, relations existing among persons, in addition to the mutual relations existing in the interactions. Thought and action structures influence the direction of competence development, which in turn will influence long-term development of social systems (see North, 1990:78).

Expectations can be driven by two main groups of functions: Cognitive expectations and normative expectations. Cognitive factors can be e.g. preferences linked do personal interests which can be expressed in laws and rules. Normative factors can e.g. be group norms, culture, ideology, integrity rumour, etc.

When cognitive expectations or normative expectations are emphasised, this depends on the situation and the context. Norms can e.g. change as a consequence of the cognitive openness on the part of the system. Therefore the degree of normative closeness and cognitive openness is an explanatory factor explaining institutional changes.

The degree of normative closeness and cognitive openness can provide guidance on how to understand the environment, how to explain the environment, and how to act in relation to the environment. Cognitive and normative expectations are therefore important to clarify.

Expectations are changed during the course of time. It can start with marginal changes, to be followed by giant leaps. Expectations with the highest degree of durability are the normative ones, and particularly the ones integrated into one's own habits. Habits are reinforced by routines, rules, traditions and conventions.

## Explaining institutional change: A pattern perspective

As shown in part I the pattern perspective emphasize the question: What is the pattern in which the behaviour take part?

It is not in fact so that the best technology will gain ground, or that competition will always further performance or lead up to the best choice. Human habits or the pattern of habits creates a historically based preference for some technologies and some situations. In this way our expectations are adjusted in relation to our habits. If this is correct, i.e. that our habits to some extent determines our use of technology, they will also be determining for the change of social systems. From the opposite perspective it could be argued that the more influence someone has on one's habits, the stronger is their normative power.

While rules can be changed quickly habits will be slower to change. Habits therefore, influence systems longer than new rules introduced in order exactly to change habits and norms. If norms are to be changed, intervention must be made at a higher level than rules, which here means to change habits. If relations among people are to be changed, this can be achieved by changing the rules that regulate the game. If lasting changes manifesting themselves in increased performance are wanted, then it is not the rules that should be changed but the habits that should be checked and changed.

Our thought and action structures can be maintained despite being unproductive, since our habits and historical attachments maintain and reinforce ways of being which obviously are not optimal. Historical attachments mean that the past has a decisive influence on our way of being here and now. These attachments also influence how changes in the environment are interpreted and what actions the individual actor will perform. Actions performed by the individual will also influence the development of stability and change in social systems. Historical attachments then influence us in relation to how we relate to technological changes, models used, and ideas and ideologies adopted by us, i.e. our pattern of behaviour.

Our thought and action structures are our constructs. They are invisible, but generate visible social consequences, through our pattern of behaviour. In this way they are of crucial importance in our attempt to change institutions and the performance in social systems.

Our thought and action patterns also influence the development of change processes in social systems. On the other hand social systems influence our institutions. This interactive (circular) understanding of change is important to gain insight into the reciprocal nature between institutions and social systems. How actors in social systems understand the thought and action room, also influences the maintenance and change of the corresponding social systems. How actors conceive of something depends on the social system they are part of. The various networks will interpret information about the environment differently. This is explained on the basis of historical factors, histories and narratives related in the network, and the entities stressed or toned down by the network. These mental models constitute both historical attachments and the various expectations in existence, our pattern of behaviour, and thus influencing and changing institutions.

Our mental models constitute our thought and action patterns. Mental processes are constituted, maintained and changed as a result of visions, i.e. the patterns of expectations we have for the future. Our visions are maintained and changed through complex interactions. Some of the important factors are however to what extent the pattern of expectations are fulfilled or not over a period of time. If expectations are not met over a period of time, the expectation mechanism will collapse. New expectations are established, which in turn will influence the vision and mental models, then being integrated in thought and action patterns, i.e. they are institutionalised, and constitute our pattern of behaviour.

Expectations can be regarded from two categories: normative

and cognitive expectations. The first one is more difficult than the other, but both influence each other. The pattern of expectations is constituted by the subjective conception of the environment on the part of each individual. Persons then select something, thereby discarding something else in the environment, when the pattern of expectation is constituted. (see North, 1990: 22 – 27). In addition to this, people's preferences over a period of time will change, which in turn will have impact on what we select and what we discard from the environment, which constitutes change.

The complexity of the environment, its pace of change, also effects change in our expectations. This comes in addition to limitations each of us has to internalise and analyse existing information.

## Conclusion

In the conclusion we will look at institutional changes in the economic partial system. We will her develop at conceptual model explaining institutional changes in the economic system. The conceptual model is at a lower abstraction level than an analytical model.

As a superior explanation factor for the economic system we

can say that expanding markets lead to increased specialization and division of work. That will in turn influence both the cognitive and normative expectations, due, among other things, to the development of new habits, new norms, new rules and new relations. This change then brings about institutional changes, which in turn will effect a direction toward new historical attachments. Specialization leads, among other things, to continuous changes and innovation. Productivity will increase and further division of work will continue, both in the individual system and between the individual systems. The increased division of work then leads to the development of coordination and integration. These functions indicate that a relatively larger part of the system's resources is spent on information processing, i.e. on developing the administrative apparatus. Further specialization and division of work pertaining to the coordination and integration function will generate a hierarchical development of systems. Both functional hierarchies and hierarchies based on symbolic distinctions are developed. These hierarchies are based on symbolic distinctions being developed. These hierarchies are then linked geographically, so that systems over a period of time will interact with each other at an increasingly higher level of structural links. In their economic consequences this leads to the development of clusters.

To handle the degree of cognitive and normative closed/open attitude, requires a focus on costs of information exchange, i.e. transaction costs, since the degree of openness versus closeness has just been linked to the boundaries of the system, and it is at the boundaries that these costs are generated. These costs increases or hinder further participation in expanding markets. Transaction costs will also influence to what extent the free market will continue to expand or not, since the alternative to the market will be other market forms. This in turn will influence the further development of specialization and division of work.

Transaction costs are decreased among other things through innovations, both technological and organizational innovations. When transaction costs are reduced, it promotes the development of expanding markets. Innovation becomes a mechanism, which during certain historical epochs will lead to economic partial systems taking new steps towards value creation, often through creative destructions. Innovation is carried out in the economic partial system, due to the inclination to achieve an innovation price at a higher level than the monopoly price. This innovation price then leads to a systematic and strategic input of new innovations to the existing market, in order to reap the innovation profit, which is higher than the monopoly profit. The market will therefore change through the continuous use of strategically marketed innovations and lead to a continuous loss of control with regards to the equilibrium of the market. After some time entrepreneurs will fill up the market with innovations generating innovation price and move the market towards equilibrium. Due to continuous innovation, propelled by the desire for innovation profit, the equilibrium will be disturbed and imbalance will be the normal situation in the market. The reason is quite simply the intention of continuously to reap the innovation profit of the market.

When the political system tries to prevent the development of monopolies, cartels, trust formations, then the economic system will expand to a higher level of abstraction, and introduce a strategy to achieve an innovation price, which at any time will be higher than the monopoly price. Economic institutional changes will be based on this understanding have precedence over changes in political, cultural and social institutions.

Referenses

**Arthur,B. (1989).** Completing technologies, increasing returns and lock in by historical events, Economic Journal, 99:116-131.

**Ashby, W.R.(1961).** An Introduction to Cybernetics. New York: Chapman & Hall LTD.

**Ashby, W.R. (1970).** Connectance of Large Dynamic (Cybernetic) Systems: Critical Values for Stability. Nature, Vol 228 no. 5273 Nov. 21.

**Ashby, W.R. (1981).** What is an Intelligent Machine? In Conant, R. (Ed.), Mechanisms of Intelligence. California: Intersystems Seaside.

**Bateson, G. (1972).** Steps to a Ecology of Mind. London: Intex Books.

**Bateson, G. (1979).** Mind and Nature. (Swedish Translation, 1988, Stockholm:Symposium & Tryckeri ).

**Bigelow, J. and Pargetter, R. (1987).** Functions, Journal of Philosophy, 84: 181-196.

**Braithwaite, R.B. (1953).** Scientific Explanation. Cambridge: Cambridge University Press.

**Bunge, M. (1967).** Scientific Research, Vol. 3, in studies of the foundations methodology and philosophy of science, Springer Verlag, Berlin.

**Bunge, M. (1983).** Exploring the World. Dordrecht: Reidel.

**Bunge, M. (1983a).** Understanding the World. Dordrecht:

Reidel.

**Bunge, M. (1985).** Philosophy of Science and Technology. Part I. Dordrecht: Reidel.

**Bunge, M. (1985a).** Philosophy of Science and Technology. Part II. Dordrecht: Reidel.

**Bunge, M. (1996).** Finding Philosophy in Social Science. New Haven CT Yale University Press.

**Bunge, M. (1997).** Mechanism and explanation. Philosophy of the Social Sciences 27: 410- 465.

**Bunge, M..(1998).** Social Science under Debate. Toronto: University of Toronto Press.

**Bunge,M. (1999).** The Sociology-Philosophy Connection. New Brunswick NJ: Transaction Publishers.

**Coase, R.H. (1988).** R.H. Coase lectures 2: The nature of the firm-Meaning, Journal of Law Economics, and organization, 4: 19-32.

**Coleman, J.S. (1991).** Constructed organization, First principles, Journal of Law Economics, and Organization, 7: 7-23.

**Eggertson, T. (1996).** A note on the economics of institutions, in Åkstan, L.J.; Eggertson, T. & North, D.C.

"Empirical studies in institutional change.pp.6-24, Cambridge University Press, Cambridge.

**Fogel, R.W. (1997).** Douglas C. North and economic theory, pp:13-29 in in J.N. Drobak & J.V.C. Nye "The frontiers of the new institutional economics, Academic Press, New York.

**Furubotn, E.G. & Richter, R. (1998).** Institutions and Economic Theory, The University of Michigan Press, Ann Arbor.

**Glaser, B.G. & Strauss, A.L. (1967).** The Discovery of Grounded Theory: Strategies for qualitative research. New York: Aldine De Gruyter.

**Hanson, N.R. (1958)**. Patterns of Discovery. Cambridge: Cambridge University Press.

**Hempel, C.G. (1965).** Aspects of Scientific Explanation. New York: Free Press.

**Kreps, D.M. (1990).** A course in microeconomic theory, Princeton University Press, Princeton.

**Kuznets, S. (1966).** Modern economic growth: Rate, structure, and spread, York University Press, New Haven.

**Langlois, R.N. (1989).** What was wrong with the old institutional economics (and what is still wrong with the new)?, Review of Political Economy, 1 (Nov.):270-298.

**Malinowski, B. (1954).** Magic, Science and Religion, and other Essays. Garden City: Doubleday Anchor Books.

**Maruyama, M. (1963).** The Second Cybernetics: Deviation Amplifying Mutual Causal Processes, American Scientist, 51: 164-179.

**Merton, R.K. (1957).** Social Theory and Social Structure. New York:

Free Press.

**Miller, J. (1978).** Living Systems, McGraw-Hill, New York.

**Miller, J.G. & Vollman, T.E. (1985).** The hidden factory, Harvard Business Review, 55, 5: 142-150.

**Nagel, E. (1956).** A Formalization of Functionalism. In Nagel, E. (Ed.), Logic Without Metaphysics: 247-283. Glencoe: Free Press.

**Nagel, E. (1961).** The Structure of Science: Problems in the Logic of Scientific Explanation. New York: Harcourt, Brace & World.

**Nagel, E. (1977).** Teleology Revisited, Journal of Philosophy, 74: 261-301.

**North, D.C. (1968).** Sources of productivity change in ocean shipping 1600-1850, Journal of Political economy, 76: 953-970.

**North, D.C. (1981).** Structure and change in economic history, Norton, New York.

**North, D.C. (1990).** Institutions, institutional change and economic performance, Cambridge University Press, Cambridge.

**North, D.C. (1994).** Economic performance through time, American Economic Review, 84: 359-368.

**North, D.C. (1996).** Epilogue: Economic performance through time. In Alston, L.J.; Eggertson, T. & North, D.C. "Empirical studies in institutional change", Cambridge University Press, Cambridge (pp.342-355).

**North, D.C. (1997).** Prologue, 3-13 in J.N. Drobak & J.V.C. Nye "The frontiers of the new institutional economics, Academic Press, New York.

**North, D.C. & Davis, L.E. (1971).** Institutional change and american economic growth, Cambridge University Press, New York.

**North, D.C. & Thomas, R.P. (1973).** The rise of the western world, The University Press, Cambridge, MA.

**Radcliffe-Brown, A.R. (1952).** Structure and Function in Primitive Society. London: Cohen and West Ltd.

**Rosenblueth, A., Wiener, N. & Bigelow, J. (1943).** Behavior,

Purpose and Teleology, Philosophy of Science, 10: 18-24.

**Salmon, W.C. (1989).** Four Decades of Scientific Explanation. In Kitcher, P. and Salmon, W.C. (eds.), Scientific Explanation: Minnesota Studies in the Philosophy of Science: 3-220. Vol. XIII. Minneapolis: University of Minnesota Press.

**Scott, R.W. (1995).** Institutions and organizations, Sage, London.

**Williamson, O.E. (1975).** Market and Hierarchies: Analysis and antitrust implications, Free Press, New York.

**Williamson, O.E. (1996).** The mechanisms of governance, Oxford University Press, Oxford.

**Wright, L. (1976).** Teleological Explanations. London:University of California Press.

# Part IV Change in society

## Chapter 4  Change from industrial society to knowledge society

## Introduction

The term "knowledge-based organizations" is used here to mean an organization that is "composed largely of specialists who direct and discipline their own performance through organized feedback from colleagues, customers, and headquarters" (Drucker, 1988: 3). Such an organization "is structured around information, not hierarchy"(Maciarello, 2014:71).  As far as we are aware, the term "knowledge worker" was used  by Drucker first in 1959 (Drucker, 1959:122).  Berger provides a definition of "knowledge worker" that gives the term the same meaning as ascribed to it by Drucker and Maciarello; that is, that knowledge workers are "people whose occupations deal with the production and distribution of symbolic knowledge"(Berger, 1987:66).

There are many examples of knowledge-based organizations: modern hospitals, symphony orchestras, universities, consultancies, engineering firms, architectural practices, etc.

The main function of a manager in a knowledge-based organization is to coordinate the flow of information between experts, and to ensure efficiency in work processes targeted at customers, users, patients etc. (Maciarello, 2014:71). A manager in such an organization does not need to possess an expert's highly specialized knowledge, but he or she must be able to communicate with experts using their professional language (Bohlander et al., 2001). In order to do this, a manager must possess contextual confidence. The manager does not need to have the same level of competence as the people he or she will manage, but he or she must have an understanding of, and be intimately acquainted with, the context (Vallima & Hoffman, 2008). Contextual confidence will enable the manager to ensure that the intended function of the system is implemented: that the organization's primary tasks are coordinated and implemented with maximum efficiency, and that everyone's capacity to perform is exploited to the full (Beer, 1995).

In addition, a manager in a knowledge-based organization must have the ability to analyse such information as is necessary for the organization to perform. He or she must also be able to communicate this information to employees (Brockbank & Ulrich, 2006).

The knowledge workers must understand what is being

communicated so that they can act in the light of this information (Maciarello, 2014:72). Drucker emphasizes the point that it is necessary to have the ability to communicate information to those who will be able to apply it most appropriately and productively (Drucker, 1999; 1999a). The point of contextual confidence is that it will enable the manager to communicate appropriate information in an understandable manner. Otherwise, while the information may be completely correct, it may be completely useless for the recipient.

Early in this debate, Savage (1995) pointed out that the advent of the knowledge society was an event equivalent to the advent of the agricultural society, or the industrial society. In the knowledge society, information will be capable of rapid transformation into resources that can by applied for value creation (Castelfranchi, 2007). The knowledge society is dependent on the existence of new technology, both ICT and the internet (Vallima & Hoffman, 2008; UNESCO, 2005). While information may be transformed into knowledge that may be used in value-creation processes, it is also true that knowledge not applied in a process that is subject to reflection and critical thinking may be counterproductive for value creation (Innerarity, 2012). A key characteristic of the knowledge society is the status of knowledge as the central commodity that is exchanged for economic prosperity. Just as agricultural goods were the key characteristic of the agricultural society, and industrial goods the key characteristic of the industrial society, so is knowledge the primary commodity of the knowledge society (Burton-Jones, 1999). Accordingly, the knowledge worker is the main class of worker in the knowledge society, just as the industrial worker was in the industrial society and the agricultural worker in the agricultural society (Drucker, 1969; 1988; 1993; 1999; 1999a).

As knowledge becomes the most important value-creation factor in the knowledge economy, there is also growing criticism of the prioritization of knowledge (Gross, 2010). There was similar criticism, however, during the transition from the agricultural society to the industrial society, when those who felt their position was under threat took to destroying industrial machines (Bowden, 1965:73). It is reasonable to anticipate that people who feel themselves threatened by the knowledge society are those who do not have the same access to knowledge processes and feel they are being marginalized (Sennet, 1998; 2013). These people will probably counteract, ignore and minimize the significance of knowledge (Guest, 2007).

The global knowledge economy is a result of globalization (Hamel, 2012). Globalization has many different aspects. One is an expansion of the concept of free trade (Santos & Williamson, 2001). Another is the emergence of new spheres of knowledge (Ulrich, 2013). One way of looking at the expansion of free trade and the development of new knowledge is to consider our analytical models, which are based on the concept of the nation state, as undergoing change (see Bauman, 1992:65).

One view proposed by Marr (1995), which concerns the development of globalization and knowledge enterprises, is that the deregulation of the money market during the 1980s accelerated globalization because it put an end to national autonomy. Hirst (1993) and Hutton (1995) take a different view. They see the expanding market as an important driving force in the development of globalization. Another way of looking at growing globalization is to consider China opening up to foreign capital at the end of the 20th century and the fall of the Berlin Wall in 1989. As a result of these two events, approximately 1.5 billion people entered the capitalist market.

What is new about the knowledge society, in our understanding, is that production has moved from classical industrial production in the industrial society to high-technology production based on new knowledge resources, new organizational methods and new technologies in the knowledge society (White & Younger, 2013). The new knowledge workers are those who, among other things, add content to what many of us access on a daily basis in the form of knowledge resources on the internet. In Europe alone, these people comprise approximately seven million knowledge workers (Jemielniak, 2012; UNESCO, 2005). These are knowledge workers who value creative processes and who are result-oriented (Drucker, 1999a).

Unlike industrial workers, knowledge workers do not appear to identify themselves with other knowledge workers as a collective phenomenon (Sennet, 1998; 2004; 2006). They identify with their own results, opportunities and expectations, not unlike an entrepreneur or an owner of capital (see Thurow, 1999).

In the industrial society, the infrastructure emerged as a crucial factor in value creation, and included the transport of goods and energy. In the knowledge society, there is much to suggest that it is the information structure, hereafter referred to as the *infostructure*, which will be a crucial factor in value creation.

The infostructure is important for information, communications and knowledge processes, as well as for "connectance" in large dynamic systems (Ashby, 1970). Amongst other things, the infostructure enables distances and borders to be reduced and diminished. This applies to geographical, psychological, cultural and social distances and borders (Baird & Henderson, 2001). Consequently, the infostructure directly affects transactions in and across different organizations (Williamson, 2013). The development of the infostructure affects the arranging of activities within and between organizations (Boxall & Purcell, 2010).

James G. Miller (1978) was one of the first to develop a theory for infostructures in social systems. Together with his research team, he examined eleven information processes (infostructure) in a social system, which we have tried to illustrate here using symbols in Fig. 2.

In addition to the infostructure, what we term the front line (i.e. those who are in contact with customers, users, citizens, patients, students, etc.) will have greater significance for value creation in individual businesses (Hannah et al., 2015). The rationale is that customers have increased competence and expect to meet someone who has equal or equivalent competence (Drucker, 1999; 1999a). Another reason is related to the fact that customers and suppliers will increasingly participate in innovation processes, more so than previously (Ramaswamy & Ozcan, 2014).

In order for the front line to be an important factor for value creation in an individual business, it is crucial that it is designed to identify and use signals and information that can be used for creativity, innovation and continuous quality improvement of the business's products and services (Jemielniak, 2012).

Creative processes are driven by competition in the global economy, where visions and expectations aimed at creating that which is new are important for value creation (Hamel, 2002; 2012); consequently, social systems will be greatly changed (Sennet, 1998; 2013). Social earthquakes will occur at both the local level of the individual, and globally for larger groups of people (see Luttwak, 1999; Sennet, 1998). Cost pressures and extreme competition will lead to a fragmentation of work processes (Hannah et al., 2015; Albrow, 1999). This fragmentation reflects an extreme specialization, which we here term a modulization of work processes (Garud et.al., 2002). This is the result of work processes being distributed, changes in organizational boundaries and the use of global partners and contractors (Drucker, 1988). The modulization of work processes increases the focus on global competence networks (Michaels et al., 2001), resulting in the manufacture of products using global rather than local expertise. These global competence networks are important for value creation in the new knowledge economy (Ramaswamy & Ozcan, 2014). Underlying factors for global competence networks are increased individualization and de-emphasising collective solutions (Sennett, 1998; 2004).

Competence in the knowledge society is a significant factor in the production process (see Boisot, 1998). It is largely rooted in global networks (see Shapiro & Varian, 1999), where extreme global specialization, focusing on core processes and competencies, is emphasised to a greater extent than previously (Tapscot & Williams, 2006). Control of development, exchange and integration of knowledge is therefore a central management mechanism for value creation processes in knowledge-based organizations (Santor & Williamson, 2001). This also implies a transition from Porter's focus on industrial clusters (Porter, 2004) to a greater emphasis on global competence networks and clusters. These global competence networks will be geographically anchored at various places around the world but are connected and integrated by new technology (Mongkhonvanit, 2010:1950). The global clusters of competence seem to direct attention towards the productivity of knowledge workers, because it is they who are responsible for most of the value creation in global knowledge businesses. In this context, identity seems to veer away from the collective towards the development of the individual knowledge worker's expertise and their own motives and needs (Drucker, 1999; 1999a). In such a situation, social contracts based on the responsibility of the collective become less prominent (Sennet, 1998; 2004; 2006; 2013). This development leads to an increased focus on the productivity of knowledge workers (Drucker, 1999; 1999a), which, it seems reasonable to assume, will lead to further modulization of economic activities and processes, and promote individual solutions at the expense of collective ones (Pyöriä, 2005). Although the focus turns more toward the individual, it is not necessarily the case that this will lead to increased respect, responsibility and dignity of the individual (Sennett, 2004).

Our understanding of globalization and the knowledge society is that they are a natural continuation of the industrial society. The new knowledge society involves new technology, new ways of organizing, new global competence clusters, and new knowledge workers who were not visible to the same extent in the industrial society. In other words, we view the knowledge society as a natural continuation of the modern society rather than a postmodern construction, which agrees with Bauman's view (Bauman, 2011).

Our fundamental assumption, which we have presented in the introduction, is that the interaction between the four elements of infostructure, front line focus, modular flexibility, and global clusters of competence, promote value creation processes in knowledge-based organizations.

The phenomenon we examine here is the transition from the industrial society to a society increasingly based on knowledge resources. The question we ask is: What are the key value creation processes in a knowledge-based organization? The first aim is to understand and explain the social mechanisms and the related social processes that influence the development of knowledge-based organizations. The second aim is to investigate what implications this development will have for management roles in the future.

Fig. 1 summarizes the introduction, and shows how the chapter is organized.

Fig. 1: Key value creation processes in the knowledge economy.

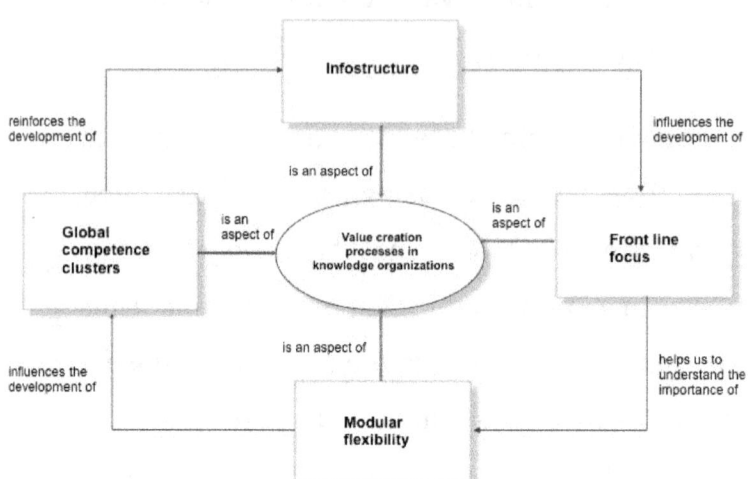

## Infostructure

The infostructure concerns the processes that enable the development, transfer, analysis, storage, coordination and management of data, information and knowledge. The infostructure consists of eleven generic processes, as shown in Fig. 2 (Miller, 1978).

The infostructure forms the basis for communication processes and the development of knowledge. It is also highly instrumental in establishing new networks on a global scale (Baird & Henderson, 2001). It is precisely the development of the new infostructure that enables new global cooperation networks as well as new organizational and leadership forms (Tapscott &

Williams, 2006). While the infrastructure facilitates the transport of goods, services and energy, the infostructure coordinates and integrates information resources on a large scale (Ramaswamy & Ozcan, 2014).

The eleven processes in the infostructure may be considered as nodes in a social network at different levels, for example team, organization, society, and region, all in the global space. Together, the eleven processes comprise the totality of the infostructure (Haag et al., 2012). The purpose of the nodes is to coordinate information so that social interaction is facilitated and new knowledge developed. The idea is that when the nodes in such a social global network co-create new knowledge and innovation is developed (Hamel, 2012).

The assumption is that in the transition from an industrial to a knowledge economy, the centre of gravity for employment shifts (Tapscot & Williams, 2006). In the knowledge society, knowledge workers perform specialized functions related to the eleven information processes in the infostructure (Reinhart et. al., 2011). Specialization within each of the eleven information processes leads to the production of knowledge in cooperating global competence clusters

(Garud & Langlois, 2002).

Each of these eleven infostructure processes is strategically important for knowledge-based organizations (Castelfranchi, 2007). Dominance of one or more of these processes allows for the possibility of control over value creation in the knowledge society (Hamel, 2012). Through control of individual processes, one has the opportunity to influence activities in other processes (Davenport, 2005). The various processes have their relative importance for value creation in the various social systems (Boisot, 1998). At the same time, they have different emphasis depending on the level that is being focused on.

Proposition 1: In the knowledge organization there will be a change in emphasis from infrastructure to the infostructure.

Management implications: The greater the emphasis on the infostructure in relation to skills development and employment, the more incomprehensible changes will seem in the social systems to those exposed to these changes, as well as the change of functional areas and competence.

Change

Social implications: The development of the infostructure may be understood as a systemic and radical innovation. It is radical because it has serious consequences for so many people around the globe. It affects almost every individual's working and private life. It is systemic because it is interconnected at many different levels, and changes in one place will affect change processes elsewhere because there is a large degree of "connectance" (Ashby, 1970).

Fig. 2 shows a schematic diagram of the infostructure processes. These processes relate to Miller (1978), but are conceptualized by us.

Fig. 2. Infostructure processes

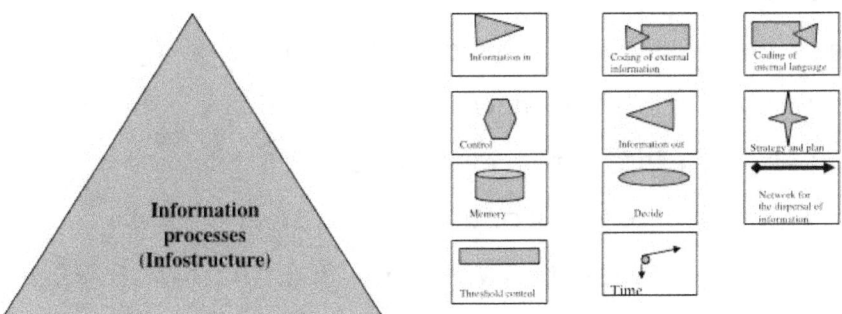

An example of a system that has been especially affected by the change in emphasis from infrastructure to the infostructure is the postal service in various countries. As the emphasis in social development began to emphasize the infostructure with a relative de-emphasis of the infrastructure, parts of the postal functions were taken over by other information carriers. An example of this is email in various networking solutions, which is represented in Fig. 2 by the symbol *network for the dispersal of information*. The consequences of this for postal services have included both the closure of post offices and the dismissal of many employees, as well as the change of functional areas and competence. The main development was a greater emphasis on various information processes as shown schematically in Fig. 2.

How the knowledge society develops is not immediately apparent, because its production processes do not follow the logic of the industrial society (Hamel, 2012; Tapscott & Williams, 2006). The production logic of the industrial society is being replaced by the new and different production logic of the knowledge society. The new logic is created by creative production on the internet, an extreme focus on innovation, and a situation where global competence clusters replace local industrial clusters (Tapscott & Williams, 2006; Thurow, 1999). One of the consequences is a stronger focus on the infostructure, and thereby a decrease in the industrial production logic framed by among others Michael Porter (Porter, 1998; 2004).

Where one is placed within the infostructure is important with regard to the impact and influence one has within the organization. This position, coupled to the goals of the organization, i.e. what it is designed to do (Beer, 1995), is decisive for determining the influence one has within the organization (Innerarity, 2012).

When the competence of customers increases, it is reasonable to assume that they expect to meet high levels of competence in their dealings with the organization. This can lead to a shift of focus in the organization logic of knowledge-based organizations, from hierarchical positions to the front line. The front line in organizations consists of those people who are in close contact with customers, users, suppliers etc. (Jemielniak, 2012). If this assumption is correct, the development of both the infostructure and focus on the front line will lead to major consequences for the role of management in the future.

Front line focus

If it is correct that information and communication processes are essential for value creation in the knowledge society, which

Reinhart et al. (2011) claim, competence in the front line will be crucial for efficient organizations. It is in dealings with customers that these processes can culminate in that which is creatively new, and where knowledge is transformed into value creation for the customer (Hamel, 2012). This can also be derived from both theory and practice related to open innovation processes (Chesbrough et al., 2008). The rationale is that the competent customer will prefer the competent supplier (Prahalad & Krishnan, 2008). A necessary condition to achieve this is that the bureaucratic structures are deconstructed, and competence, service, information and decisions are moved to the front line (Hannah et al., 2015). If this doesn't occur, it could hinder restructuring and be a costly element of knowledge-based organizations (Jemielniak, 2012).

Creativity and innovation are prerequisites for value creation in the knowledge society (Prahalad & Krishnan, 2008; Hamel, 2012). Bureaucracy, with its stabilizing thought mode, has difficulty in adapting to rapid changes because change dynamics are not bureaucracy's primary thought mode (Bauman, 2011).

The bureaucratic model was effective for its time, where stability was the primary focus. In the knowledge society, however, change processes are the primary mode because globalization, rapidity of information processes, focus on innovation, and the rapid spread of innovation lead to dynamic change processes (Prahalad & Krishnan, 2008). Creative destruction will probably be normal in such a situation because the pace of change increases in the global knowledge economy (Hamel, 2012). This could lead to demand for major reorganization and increasing pace of change in the industrial society (Rooney et al., 2008: 55-57; 160-161).

A common feature of the knowledge society seems to crystallize as structural links, or "connectance" in Ashby's model (Ashby, 1970). It seems possible that continuous changes in structural connections will lead to customers' expectations, wants and needs changing (Ramaswamy & Ozcan, 2014). Coping with these continuous changes presupposes that organizations have sufficient variety in their capabilities so that they can match customers' competencies, which is related to the "law of requisite variety" (Ashby, 1970). It is reasonable to assume that the capability must exist where the customer interacts with the business - in the front line. Sufficient competence in the front line, satisfying customers' requirements, will be a decisive competitive factor for businesses (Nordhaug, 1994). If competence in the front line is crucial, and the front line is largely identical with where decisions are taken, perhaps bureaucratic structures will be less important for decision-making processes in knowledge based organizations (Davenport, 2005).

Competence in the front line, collective learning structures between businesses, customers and suppliers, and flexibility as a structuring mode will in such an organization be key creation processes (Hannah et al., 2015).

Requisite variety in competence, in relation to the individual customer, presupposes an information system in the front line that focuses on continuous change in the customer's needs and wants. In addition, the organization will have a competitive advantage when they have an organizational learning system that focuses on interaction between the organization, the customer and supplier (Haag et al., 2012). Businesses that are able to change their form of organization to a focus on the front line, and develop work processes connected to new technology that focus on cooperation in the global clusters of competence will be in the forefront of the global knowledge economy (Hamel, 2012; Jemielniak, 2012).

Proposition 2: Competence, service, information and decisions are moved to the front line in the knowledge organization.

Management implications: A necessary condition to achieve front line focus, is that the hierarchical and bureaucratic structures are deconstructed.

Social implications: Creativity and innovation are prerequisites for value creation in the knowledge society, and creative destruction will probably be normal.

The frontline focus helps us to understand the necessity and importance of modular flexibility (Garud et al., 2002), which we will elaborate on in the next section. A figurative presentation of the discussion in this section is shown in Fig. 3.

Fig. 3. Frontline focus

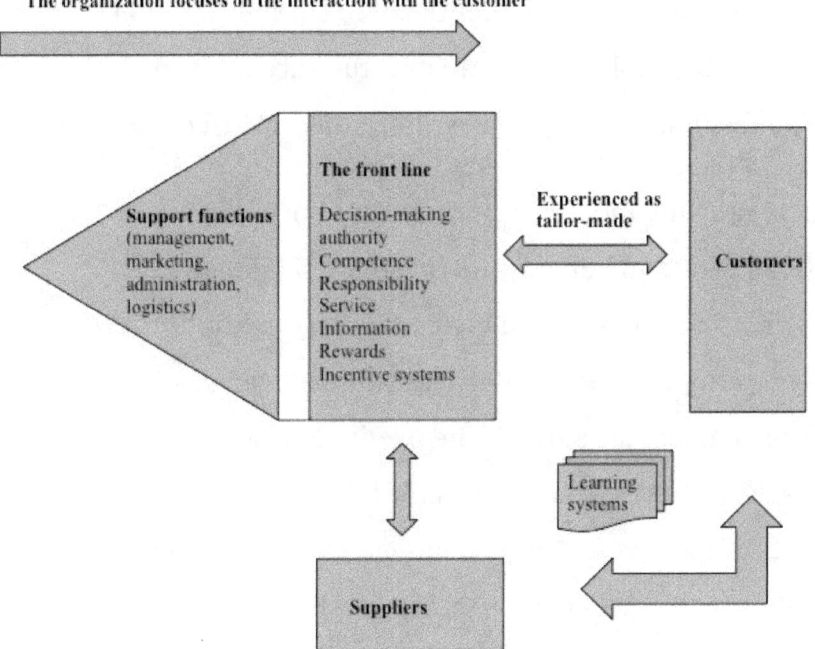

## Modular flexibility

The modulization of value creation is termed here modular flexibility (Garud et al., 2002). Modular flexibility may best be understood as the globalization of production processes, and extreme specialization of work processes with a focus on core processes (Gershuny & Fisher, 2014). Of course, the economist Adam Smith as early as 1776 described a similar process when he delineated the structured activities of a pin factory. What is new in the global knowledge economy is that modular thinking is systematised on an unprecedented global scale, and that currently new technology and infostructure are used to streamline this modular logic (Brynjolfsson & McAfee, 2014).

The new organising modus is characterised by classical industrial production being re-integrated into global modules, in accordance with a logic of costs, quality, competence and innovation (Karabarbounis & Neiman, 2013). This means that parts of the production will move to areas where costs, such as for labour, are low. Other parts of the production are moved to areas where they have a specific expertise, for instance Banglore in India in the case of IT expertise. Other parts of the production are moved to areas known for design and innovation expertise (Autor et al., 2003).

Metaphorically, this may be understood as a form of organization based on a "Lego principle": the individual Lego bricks are produced where they have the necessary expertise or where costs are low. Finally, the product is assembled where they have a special competence in understanding the totality of the product. Modular global manufacturing is unified and coordinated using new ICT. In other words, it may be imagined that the overall design of the product is ready (Azmat et al., 2012; Hsieh & Klenow, 2007).

Those who feel the pressure in such a structure are the industrial workers in welfare states where wages and working conditions have been negotiated over a long period of time, and are thus not competitive in relation to low-cost countries (Acemoglu, 2003: 1-37). Low-cost countries, however, can still have a highly skilled workforce and thus produce high-quality products. As mentioned, an example of this is Bangalore, India. Bangalore is the capital of the state of Karnataka. It has more than four million inhabitants and, amongst others, specializes in the education of software engineers. This example shows that it is not only unskilled and skilled labour that is ousted in the global economy, but also highly skilled knowledge workers in Western industrialized countries (Brynjolfsson & McAfee, 2014).

The logical consequence of specialization and division of labour is that it becomes progressively global, increasing competition and forcing down costs (Rios-Rull & Santaeulalia-Llopis, 2010). However, the globalization of labour and other costs leads to an increase in social conflicts (Sennett, 1998). This is, amongst other things, a consequence of established salary structures being exposed to global competition (Innerarity, 2012).

Proposition 3: Modular thinking is systematised on an unprecedented global scale

Management implication: The production system is moved in the global sphere in accordance with a logic of costs, -quality, -competence and –innovation.

Social implication: The industrial workers in welfare states will suffer.

In fig. 4 we have shown the modular logic we described in this section.

## Fig. 4 Modular logic

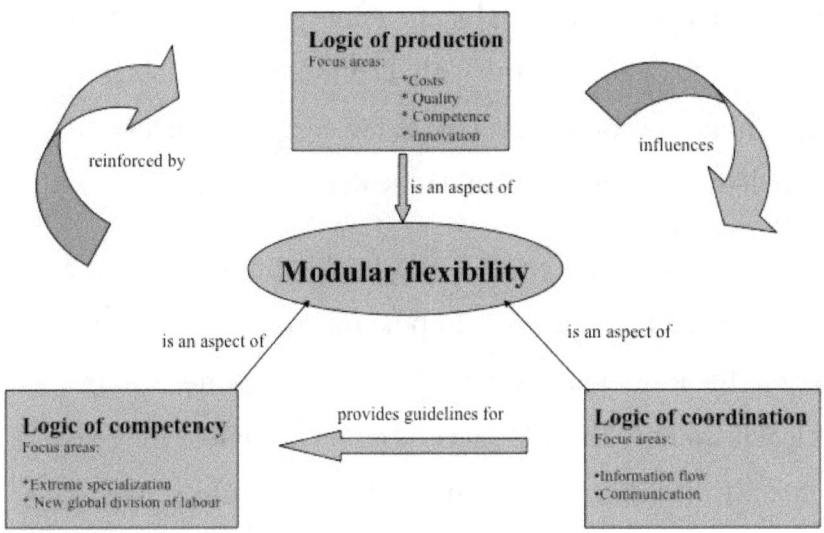

*Global competence clusters*

Porter (1998) argues that economic growth is largely created through local business clusters. The new technology, however, promotes a new logic of information, communication and networking in the globalized knowledge economy (Brynjolfsson & McAfee, 2014). This new logic, coupled to the fact that expertise is increasingly becoming a global resource (Autor & Murnane, 2003) available in the new infostructure, makes the global competence networks important forces in value creation (Fisher, 2006). This development promotes the idea that global clusters of competence, to a greater extent than the local clusters, are crucial for the development of innovation and economic growth (Ramaswamy & Ozcan, 2014). From such a standpoint, local business clusters may be understood in the context of the global competence clusters when explaining the complexities of value creation processes in the knowledge economy (Prahalad & Krishnan, 2008).

Structurally linked competence networks that are spread globally may constitute the most important value creation structures in the knowledge society (Auto & Murnane, 2003; Gershuny & Fisher, 2014). Global competence clusters may be geographically distributed at the individual level and consist of small, tightly-knit social networks, or be small groups with expertise; these are structurally connected through the new infostructure (Brynjolfsson & McAfee, 2014). In this way, global expertise is fully utilized for innovation and economic growth (Ramaswamy & Ozcan, 2014). In other words, the global competence clusters can be viewed together with the local clusters, and it may be imagined that the connection between the two can prove to be the main drivers of value creation in the knowledge society in the future (Acemoglu, 2003). In this context, it is the structural links that are of interest, not the local clusters or global competence networks separately.

From this viewpoint, the knowledge society and globalization mark a transition from a focus on local business clusters to a focus on links between global competence networks and local clusters with regards to value creation. This also leads to increased co-creation, interconnectedness and connectance (Ashby, 1970); these three concepts are linked to the idea that in some contexts collaboration is important, while in others competition is more crucial (Ramaswamy & Ozcan, 2014). In continuation of this trend, there is a transition from a focus on power and bureaucracy in a hierarchical system to a focus on trust and cooperation across ethnic boundaries and an emphasis on relationships in the global competence network (Sennett, 2013).

New technologies, innovation developed through global competence clusters, infostructure, modular flexibility and front line focus all serve to promote and enable the production of goods and services that can be distributed modularly in the global knowledge economy. The infostructure enables all the information that can be sent over a global network to be accessed, analysed, stored, recovered and transferred from places that can compete on cost, quality, expertise and innovation.

Co-creation is important for knowledge, knowledge transfer and knowledge integration (Ramaswamy & Ozcam, 2014; Tapscot & Williams, 2006). Co-creation involves working together to promote knowledge processes and innovation. Although competition has proven to promote productivity and economic growth, it is not necessarily this factor that should be emphasized in the global competence network. Pfeffer & Sutton (1999: 102) express this as follows: "There is a mistaken idea that because competition has apparently triumphed as an economic system, competition within organizations is a similar superior way of managing." In other words, although competition promotes productivity and economic growth in the industrial society, it is not certain that the same mechanisms apply to knowledge development and sharing in the knowledge society.

Competence development presupposes just as much cooperation in the global competence network as it does competition. The constant interaction between competition and cooperation results in co-creation becoming increasingly important for value creation. This may prove to be the fundamental driving force for value creation in the knowledge society (Ramaswamy & Ozcam, 2014). The thinking in this context is that if competition is the only prevailing principle, then everyone will protect their ideas from disclosure and knowledge development will be inhibited. If collaboration is the only principle driving the development of knowledge forward, then it seems reasonable to assume that motivation and incentives will not be optimal for the development of new knowledge. The balance between competition and cooperation, embodied in the concept of co-creation, leads to constructive criticism and the necessary scope of knowledge that exists in the network so as to promote creativity and the innovative. Instead of a zero-sum situation, a positive-sum situation will be developed where everyone wins.

Co-creation is connected to developing complementary competence teams in a global competence network. In such a social network, mentoring, cross-functional teams and collaborative teams may be developed across cultural and physical boundaries (Sennett, 2013). In addition, this presupposes a culture in which the success of colleagues is viewed as the success of the system. Shapiro & Varian (1999: 10) also emphasize the importance of focusing on cooperation in the networked economy: "...the need for collaboration, and the multitude of cooperative arrangements has never been greater than in the area of infotech". An example of the importance of co-creation is the necessity of working together to develop standards for technology and system integrations, while competing for the products and services that will be delivered using these established standards. If there is a failure to agree on standards, innovation may be hampered and value creation and economic growth may suffer as a consequence. In such a situation, the users and customers are the losers. The example concerning the development of standards shows that *cooperation is a prerequisite for competition*, in the same way as change is a prerequisite for stability. It is always a balance between competition and cooperation that creates good solutions, like the tight rope acrobat who has to find a balance between change and stability, moving his/her arms and legs in order to maintain overall stability while walking along the tight rope.

Proposition 4: Global clusters of competence, to a greater extent than the local clusters, are crucial for the development of value creation in knowledge organizations.

Management implications: There will be a transition from a focus on local business clusters to a focus on links between global competence networks and local clusters with regards to value creation.

Social implications: If global clusters of competence are essential for value creation in the knowledge society, co-creation is an important social mechanism for initiating, maintaining and strengthening these processes.

## Conclusion

The chapter's research question: *What are the key value creation processes in a knowledge-based organization?*

The chapter has stressed the importance of five elements:

1. A new emphasis on the infostructure
2. A new way of organizing businesses, termed here a front line focus
3. A new way of structuring work processes, termed here modular flexibility
4. A new way of using competence, termed here global competence clusters


A focus on the frontline will promote a new kind of leader who does not have a position in the hierarchy, but has the same management functions in relation to customers as the hierarchical leader had previously. These people have high competence and are characterized by their ability to embrace simplicity.

The emphasis of the new infostructure, modular flexibility and global competence clusters requires leaders who can handle extreme complexity.

The restructuring of the world economy which follows

from, amongst other things, new technologies, new structures of cooperation, global competence networks, modulization of production, and a front line focus may lead to a polarization between information-rich and information-poor systems at various system levels.

In the global economy, new geographical areas will be drawn into the economic dynamics, while other areas will be marginalized. Marginalization will result in these areas becoming economic backwaters, where value creation processes are not in tune with the global economy. Social exclusion, greater economic differences and a greater degree of individualization seem to be some of the consequences of the future global knowledge economy. For the world economy, areas that are located in the infostructure's backwater will be of little interest and not economically relevant. These areas, whether they are organizations, nations or regions, will be excluded from value creation processes. In 2013, only 39 percent of the world's population had access to the internet (Sanou, 2013). This says something both about the potential of value creation, but also about exclusion from value creation processes.

The same processes of social sanctioning, exclusion and reproduction of social inequality occur on both local and global levels. On the other hand, the flow of information pulls other areas up to economic affluence, abundance and sometimes conspicuous consumption. This polarization seems to be one of the characteristics of the knowledge society (see Castells, 1997: 70-166). Another characteristic, according to Castells (1997: 70-166), is that rich social networks are connected via mutually reinforcing value creation structures. However, we have a need for more knowledge about both value creation processes in the individual knowledge-based organizations and also in the global economy, and what the transition from infrastructure to the infostructure means to value creation on the various system levels.

References

**Acemoglu, D. (2003).** Labor-and Capital-Augmenting Technical Change, Journal of European Economic Association, 1, 1:1-37.

**Albrow, M.** (1999). The global age, Stanford University Press, CAL.

**Ashby, W.R. (1970).** Connectance of Large Dynamic

(Cybernetic) Systems: Critical Values for Stability. Nature, Vol 228 no. 5273 Nov. 21.

**Axford, B. (1995).** The global system: Economics, politics and culture, Polity Press, Cambridge.

**Autor, D.; Levy, F. & Murnane, R.J. (2003).** The Skill Content of recent technological change: An empirical exploration, The Quarterly Journal of Economics, Vol. 118, no. 4, pp. 1279-1333.

**Azmat, G.; Manning, A. & Van Reenen, J. (2012).** Privatization and the Decline of the Labour's Share: International Evidence from Network Industries, Economica, 79:470-492.

**Baird, L. & Henderson, J.C. (2001).** The Knowledge Engine, Berrett-Koehler, San Francisco.

**Bauman, Z. (1992).** Intimitations of postmodernity, Routledge, London.

**Bauman, Z. (2011).** Culture in a liquid modern world, Polity Press, London.

**Beer, S. (1995).** Diagnosing the system for organizations, John Wiley & Sons, London.

**Berger, P. (1987).** The capitalist revolution: Fifty propositions about prosperity, equality and liberty, Basic Books, New York.

**Boisot, M. (1998).** Knowledge Assets: Securing Competitive Advantage in the

Information Economy, Oxford University Press, Oxford.

**Bohlander,G.; Snell, S. & Sherman, A. (2001).** Managing Human Resources, South Western College Publishing, Cincinnati,OH.

**Bowden, W. (1965).** Industrial Society in England, Routledge, London.

**Boxall,P.F. & Purcell, J. (2010).** An HRM perspective on Employee Participation, in Wilkinson, A.; Golan, P.J.; Marchington, M.& Lewins, D. (eds.). The Oxford Handbook of Participation in Organizations, Oxford University Press, Oxford, s. 129-151.

**Brockbank, W. & Ulrich, D. (2006).** Higher Knowledge for Higher Aspirations, Human Resource Management Journal, 44:4:489-504.

**Brynjolfsson, E. & McAfee, A. (2014).** The Second machine Age, W.W. Noron, New York.

**Burton-Jones, A. (1999).** Knowledge Capitalism: Business, Work, and Learning in the New Economy, Oxford University Press, Oxford.

**Castelfranchi, C. (2007).** Six critical remarks on science and the construction of the knowledge society. Journal of Science Communication, 6(4), 1-3.

**Castells, M. (1997).** The information age: Economy, society and culture, Vol II: The power of identity,

**Chang, S-J. (2008).** Sony vs. Samsung: The inside story of the electronic giants battle for global supremacy, John Wiley and Sons, Singapore.

**Chesbrough, H.; vanhavebeke, W. & West, J. (2008).** Open Innovation: Researching a New Paradigm, OUP, Oxford.

**Cortada, James W. (1998).** Rise of the Knowledge Worker, Butterworth-Heinemann, Boston.

**Davenport, T. H. (2005).** Thinking for a Living, How to Get Better Performance and Results from Knowledge Workers, Harvard Business School Press, Boston.

**Drucker, P.F. (1959).** Landmarks of Tomorrow, Heinemann, New York.

**Drucker, P.F. (1969).** The age of discontinuity: Guidelines to our changing society, Harper & Row, New York.

**Drucker, P.F. (1986).** The changed world economy, Foreign Affairs, 64: 768-791.

**Drucker, P. (1988).** The coming of the new organization,

Harvard Business Review, 88: 45-53.

**Drucker, P (1993)** Post-Capitalist society, Butterworth, Heinemann, Oxford.

**Drucker, P.F. (1999).** Knowledge worker productivity: The biggest challenge, California management Review, 41, 2: 79-94.

**Drucker, P.F. (1999a).** Knowledge worker productivity: The biggest challenge, California management Review, 41, 2: 79-94.

**Drucker. P.F. (1999a).** Management Challenges for the 21st Century. Harper Collins, New York.

**Fisher, J.D. (2006).** The Dynamic Effects of Neutral and Investment-Specific Technology Shocks, Journal of Political Economy, 114, 3:413-451.

**Garud, R.; Kumaraswamy, A. &,Langlois, R. (2002).** Managing in the Modular Age: New Perspectives on Architectures, Networks and Organizations, Wiley-Blackwell, New York.

**Gershuny, J. & Fisher, K. (2014).** Post-industrious society: Why work time will not disappear for our grandchildren,, Center for Time Use Research, Department of Sociology, University of Oxford.

**Gross, M. (2010).** Ignorance and Surprise: Science, Society, and Ecological Design. Cambridge, MA: MIT Press.

**Guest, D.E. (2007).** HRM and the Worker: Towards a new Psychological Contract, in Boxall, P.; Purcell, J. & Wright, P.; The Oxford Handbook of Human Resource Management, Oxford University Press, Oxford. S. 128-146.

**Haag, S.; Cummings, M.; McCubbrey, D.; Pinsonneault, A.; Donovan, R. (2012).** *Management Information Systems for the Information Age*, McGraw Hill, Ryerson.

**Hamel, G. (2002).** Leading the Revolution: How to Thrive in Turbulent Times by Making Innovation a Way of Life, Harvard Business School Press, Boston.

**Hamel, G. (2012).** What matters now: How to win in a world of relentless change Ferocious Competition, and Unstoppable Innovation, John Wiley & Sons, New York.

**Hannah, E.; Scott, J.; Trommer, S. (2015).** Expert knowledge in Global Trade, Routledge, London.

**Hedberg, B. (1997).** Virtual organizations and beyond : Discover imaginary systems. New York: John Wiley & Sons.

**Hirst, P.** (1993). Globalization is fashionable but is it a myth? Guardian, 22 mars.

**Hsieh, C-T. & Kienow, P. (2007).** Relative Prices and Relative Prosperity, The American Economic Review, 97, 3:562-585.

**Hutton, W.** (1995). Myth that sets the world to right,

Guardian, 12 june, s. 17.

**Innerarity, D. (2012).** Power and knowledge: The politics of the knowledge society, European Journal of Social Theory, 16(1), 3-16.

**Jemielniak, D. (2012).** The New Knowledge Workers, Edward Elgar, Cheltenham.

**Karabarbounis, L. & Neiman, B. (2013).** The Global Decline of the Labor Share, NBER Working Paper nr. 19136.

**Luttwak, E. (1999).** Turbo capitalism, Harper, New York.

**Maciariello, J.A. (2014).** A Year With Peter Drucker, Harper Business, New York.

**Maciariello, J.A & Linkletter, K.E. (2011).** Druckers lost art of management, McGraw-Hill, New York.

**Machlup, F. (1962).** The production and distribution of knowledge in the United States, Princeton University Press, princeton, NJJ.

**Machlup, F. (1981).** Knowledge and knowledge production, Princeton University press, Princeton.

**Machlup, F. & Kronwinkler, T. (1975).** Workers who produce knowledge: A steady increase 1900 to 1970, Weltwirtschaftliches Archiv, 3: 752-759.

**Marr, A. (1995).** The real enemy is the moneymarket, Spectator, 9.sept. s. 20-21.

**Mcdermott, M. (2005).** Knowledge Workers: You can gauge their effectiveness, Leadership Excellence **22** (10): 15–17.

**Michaels, E.; Hanfield-Jones, H. & Axelrod, B. (2001).** The War for Talent, Harvard Business School Press, Boston.

**Miller, J.G. (1978).** Living systems, McGraw Hill, new York.

**Mongkhonvanit, M.J. (2010).** Industrial Cluster and Higher Education, Xlibris, London.

**Mosco, V.; McKercher, C. (2007).** Introduction: Theorizing Knowledge Labor and the Information Society. Knowledge Workers in the Information Society., Lexington Books, Lanham.

**Nordhaug, O. (1994).** Human capital in organizations: Competence, training and learning, Scandinavian University Press, Oslo.

**Pfeffer,J. & Sutton, R.J. (1999).** Knowing what to do is not enough: Turning knowledge into action, California management Review, Vol. 42,1: 83-108.

**Porter, M. (1998).** Clusters and the New Economics of Competition, Harvard Business Review, nov.-dec. Pp. 77-90.

**Porter, M. (2004).** Competitive Strategy, Free Press, New

York.

**Prahalad, C. K. & Krishnan, M.S. (2008).** The New Age of Innovation: Driving Cocreated Value Through Global Networks, McGraw-Hill, New York.

**Pyöriä, P. (2005).** The Concept of Knowledge Work Revisited. *Journal of Knowledge Management* **9** (3): 116–127

**Ramaswamy, V. & Ozcan, K. (2014).** The Co-Creation Paradigm, Stanford University Press, Stanford.

**Reinhardt, W., Smith, B.; Sloep, P.Drachler, H. (2011).** Knowledge Worker Roles and Actions – Results of Two Empirical Studies, Knowledge and Process Management **18** (3): 150–174.

**Rios-Rull, J-V. & Santaeulalia-Llopis,R. (2010).** Redistributive Shocks and Productivity Shocks, Journal of Monetary Economics, 57:931-948.

**Rooney, D.; Heam, G. & Kastelle, T. (2008).** Handbook of the Knowledge economy, Edward Elgar, New York.

**Sanou, B. (2013).** The world in 2013: ICT fact and figures. Retrieved from http://www.itu.int/en/ITUD/Statistics/Documents/facts/ICT FactsFigures2013.pdf

**Santos, D.Y. & Williamson, P. (2001).** From Global to

Metanational: How Companies Win in the Knowledge Economy, Harvard Business School Press, Boston.

**Savage, C. (1995).** Fifth Generation Management: Co-creating through Virtual Enterprising, Dynamic Teaming and Knowledge Networking, Butterworth-Heinemann, Boston.

**Sennett, R. (1998).** The Corrosion of Character: Personal Consequences of Work in the New Capitalism, W.W. Norton & Company, New York.

**Sennet, R. (2004).** Respect, Norton, New York.

**Sennet, R. (2006).** The Culture of the New Capitalism, Yale University Press, London.

**Sennett, R. (2013).** The Rituals, Pleasures and Politics of Cooperation, Penguin, London.

**Shapiro, C. & Varian, H.R. (1999).** Information rules: A strategic guide to the network economy, Harvard Business School press, Boston, Mass.

Stacey, R.D. (1996). Complexity and Creativity in Organizations, Berrett-Koehler, London.

**Tapscott, D. & Williams, A.D. (2006).** Wikinomics: How Mass Collaboration Changes Everything, Penguin, New York.

**Thurow, L. (1999).** Creating wealth, Nicolas Brealey, London.

**Ulrich, D. (2013).** Future of Global HR: What's Next?, in Ulrich, D.; Brockbank, W.; Younger, J. & Ulrich, M. (eds.), Global HR Competencies: Mastering Competitive Value from the Outside in, McGraw Hill, New York. S. 255-268.

**UNESCO (2005).** United Nations Educational, Scientific and Cultural Organization (2005). Toward knowledge societies. *UNESCO World Report*. Conde-sur-Noireau, France: Imprimerie Corlet.

**Vallima, J. & Hoffman, D. (2008).** Knowledge society discourse and higher education. Higher Education, 56(3), 265-285.

**Wegge m.fl. (2010)** artikkel hvor Hans Jeppe Jeppersen er medforfatter, artikkel bestilt

**White, J. & Younger, J. (2013).** The Global Perspective, in Ulrich, D.; Brockbank, W.; Younger, J. & Ulrich, M. (eds.); Global HR Competencies: Mastering Competitive Value from the Outside in, McGraw Hill, New York. S. 27-53.

**Williamson, O.E. (2013).** The Transaction Cost Economics Project: The Theory and Practice of Governance and Contractual Relations, Edward Elgar Publishing, New York.

# Chapter on concepts

**Ambidextrous organizations.** *Ambidextrous organizations* are organizations that have the ability to adapt to changes in external conditions while at the same time generating their own future by means of, among other things, performance improvement, growth and innovation (Duncan, 1976; O'Reilly & Tushman, 2004, 2006, 2011; Thota & Munir, 2011). In chapter 6, we have shown how ambidextrous organizations can be developed by HR departments.

In 2004, O'Reilly & Tushman expressed that ambidextrous organizations would constitute one of the major challenges for management in the global knowledge economy.

The findings of O'Reilly & Tushman (2004) were overwhelming. Regarding the launching of radical innovations, they found that none of the cross-functional or unsupported teams and only a quarter of the teams with functional designs were able to produce radical innovations. However, among the ambidextrous organizations, 90% were successful in producing radical innovations. Empirical research has shown that this type of organizational design is best for producing both incremental and radical innovations (Thora & Munir, 2011).

**Asplund's motivation theory**[1]. In brief, this theory can be described in the following way: *People are motivated by social responses* (Asplund, 2010: 221-229). The following statement may be said to be a central point made by Asplund's theory: *When people receive social responses, their level of activity increases.*

Asplund's motivation theory is consistent with North's action theory (ref. North's action theory). Understood in this way, it seems reasonable to connect the two theories in the statement: *People are motivated by the social responses rewarded by the institutional framework.*

**Availability cascades.** This refers to the idea that we are all controlled by the image of reality created by the media, because this image is easy to retrieve from memory.

**Availability proposition.** This may be expressed as follow: The more easily information enters into our consciousness, the greater the likelihood that we will have confidence in that information. In other words, we believe more in the type of

---

[1] Asplund's motivation theory, a term we use here, is based on Asplund's research..

information that is available in memory than the information that is not so readily available.

**Behavioural perspective.** This perspective focuses on the behaviour of employees as an explanation for the relationship between business strategy and the results obtained.

**Boudon-Coleman diagram.** This research methodology was developed by Mario Bunge (Bunge, 1978:76-79) based on insights made by the sociologists Boudon and Coleman. The purpose of the diagram is to show the relationship between the various levels, such as the macro and micro-levels. For instance, it is shown how changes at the macro-level, such as technological innovations in feudal society, can lead to increased income at the micro-level. However, it was shown that technological innovations could lead to weakening of the semi-feudal structures because dependency on land owners was reduced. Consequently, the landowners opposed such changes especially in the case of technological innovations, which Boudon has shown in his research (Boudon, 1981: 100). Coleman (Coleman, 1990: 7-12) started at the macro level, went to the individual level to find explanations and finally ended up at the macro level again.

An important purpose of Bunge's Boudon-Coleman diagram is to identify social mechanisms that maintain or change the phenomenon or problem under investigation (as mentioned above, in Boudon's analysis of semi-feudal society). Bunge's Boudon-Coleman diagram may be said to represent a "mixed strategy"; Bunge says the following: *When studying systems of any kind a) reduce them to their components (at some level) and the interaction among these, as well as among them and environmental items, but acknowledge and explain emergence* (see the chapter on concepts) *whenever it occurs, and b) approach systems from all pertinent sides and on all relevant levels, integrating theories or even research fields whenever unidisciplinarity proves to be insufficient* (Bunge, 1998:78). The purpose of this research strategy is to arrive at a deeper and more complete explanation of a system's behaviour.

**Capabilities**. Capabilities are for an organization what abilities are for an individual.

An organizational capability may thus be defined as an organization's ability to perform a task, activity or process. Operational capabilities enable an organization to make money in the here and now (Winter, 2003: 991-995). Dynamic capabilities, as opposed to operational capabilities, are linked to processes of change. Change and innovation are at the centre of dynamic capabilities.

Simplified, one may say that organizational capabilities are something an organization does well compared to its competitors (Ulrich and Brockbank, 2005). These capabilities are intangible and therefore difficult for competitors to imitate (Wernerfelt, 1984).

**Cohesive energy.** In a social system cohesive energy is "the glue" that binds the system together. Cohesive energy is the social mechanisms that make the system durable. According to systemic thinking it is the relationships and actions that bind social systems together. The rationale is that relationships and the systems of relationships may be said to control human behaviour. Social systems are held together (in systemic thinking) by dynamic social relations (e.g. feelings, perceptions, norms) and social action (e.g. cooperation, solidarity, conflict and communication).

**Co-creation.** Co-creation involves working together to promote knowledge processes and innovation. If knowledge processes and innovation are essential for value creation in the knowledge society, co-creation is an important social mechanism for initiating, maintaining and strengthening these processes. The balance between competition and cooperation, embodied in the concept of co-creation, leads to constructive criticism and the necessary scope of knowledge that exists in the network so as to promote creativity and the innovative. Instead of a zero-sum situation, a positive-sum situation will be developed where everyone wins.

**Collective blindness.** Collective blindness may be said to be a form of collective arrogance, which results in irrational actions. Minor events slip under the radar, causing the system to not be fully aware of what is happening. Politicians' explanations why voters in a referendum vote contrary to what most of the power elite and the media advocated is an example of collective blindness.

**Competence**. Competence refers to knowledge, skills and attitudes.

**Core Competence.** The concept was popular in the strategy literature of the 1990s. Core competence may be defined as: *"a bundle of skills and technologies that enable a company to provide a particular benefit to customers"* (Hamel & Prahalad, 1996:219). More recently, core competence as a concept has been given less attention in the research on dynamic capabilities, and now there is more focus on the concept of *fitness*. The term *evolutionary fitness* is also used in the research literature in connection with technology, quality, cost development, market development, innovation and competitive positioning (Helfat, et al, 2007: 7).

**Discontinuous innovations.** These are innovations that change the premises of technology, markets, our mindset, and so on. We know that sooner or later discontinuous innovations will emerge in the future (Hewing, 2013).

**Dynamic capabilities.** Dynamic capabilities stem from the resource-based perspective and evolutionary thinking in strategy literature (Teece, 2013: 3-65; 82-113; Nelson and Winter, 1982). The dynamic perspective attempts to explain what promotes an organization's competitive position over time through innovation and growth (Teece, 2013: x).

The original thinking concerning dynamic capabilities may be related to Teece et al. (1997). These authors defined dynamic capabilities as *an organization's ability to create, develop and modify its internal and external expertise in order to address changes in the external world.*

Dynamic capabilities are now seen as all the organizational processes, not only internal and external expertise, that contribute to an organization's capacity to adapt to change while creating the organization's future.

**Explicit knowledge.** This is knowledge that can be digitized and communicated to others as information.

**Evidence.** This may be results, such as research results, that can be relied on. However, it is also important to be aware of the fact that other evidence may be available without having to refer to figures and quantities, such as evidence that emerges from observations and good judgment without the assessment being quantified. Evidence-based research is research results that are based on approved and accepted scientific research methods.

**Emergent.** An emergent occurs if something new turns up on one level that has not previously existed on the level below. With emergent we mean: *Let S be a system with composition A, i.e. the various components in addition to the way they are composed. If P is a property of S, P is emergent with regard to A, if and only if no components in A possess P; otherwise P is to be* *regarded as a resulting property with regards to A.* (Bunge, 1977:97).

**Feedback** Giving the other person feedback, for instance with regard to their behaviour, attitudes, and the like, is the most important element in the area of interactive skills and emotional intelligence (Goleman, 1996; 2007). Analysis of feedback is a sure way to identify our strengths and then reinforce them (Wang, et al., 2003). Failure to give people feedback on their behavior in some contexts may even be considered immoral.

**Feed-forward.** Feed-forward is regarded here as an expectation mechanism. It seems reasonable to assume that our expectations influence our behaviour in the present. It is therefore important that we make explicit to ourselves the expectations we have of a situation. By making expectations explicit, we have a greater opportunity to learn from our experiences and thus improve our performance.

**Front line focus.** This refers to those in the front line, i.e. in direct contact with customers, users, patients, students, etc. They have the greatest expertise, necessary information, and decision-making authority and are regarded as the most important resource in the organization because they are at the point where an organization's value creation occurs.

**Global competence network.** These competence networks may be divided into political, social, economic, technological and cultural patterns. It is when these five patterns interact that one may perceive the overall pattern. In the global knowledge economy it seems reasonable to assume that those who control this pattern set the conditions for economic development. These global competence networks will most likely make an impact on HR departments in companies competing for this kind of expertise in national markets.

Global competence networks are also emphasized as crucial for economic growth by OECD (2001), although they use the term *innovative clusters.* The purpose of innovative clusters and global competence networks is the development, dissemination and use of new ideas that promote wealth creation.

There is much to suggest that a greater degree of integration and cooperation between private and public sectors at the national and regional levels is an important prerequisite for initiating the innovative locomotive effect. The global competence networks are metaphorically the energy source that sustains the motion of this locomotive. It would be counterproductive to replace the locomotive once in motion. Conversely, the individual carriages of the locomotive (read: organizational level) can be changed depending on their competitive position. The individual passengers on the train create ideas and knowledge through the processes that may be called *creative chaos*. In this way we will arrive at a tripartite of the prerequisites for global competence networks. At the individual level, creative chaos occurs. At the organizational level, there will be creative destruction. At the social and global levels, creative collaboration takes place. These three processes create innovation and economic growth as an emergent, not as a *future perfectum*, i.e. a planned process with given results.

A prerequisite for the reasoning above is that tension and competition at one level requires collaboration at another level. Competition and cooperation are both necessary if one is to develop innovation and economic growth, in the same manner that stability and change are necessary for flexibility. Too much of the one (stability) leads to rigidity, and too much of the other (change) leads to chaos. Understood in this way, emergents cannot be planned.

**Hamel's Law of Innovation.** The "law" states that only between one and two of one thousand ideas become innovations in a market (Hamel, 2002; 2012). Therefore, an infostructure must be created to ensure that ideas are continuously produced in a business.

**Hidden knowledge.** Hidden knowledge is what we do not know we do not know. Kirzner (1982) says that hidden knowledge is possibly the most important knowledge domain of creativity, innovation and entrepreneurship.

**History's "slow fields".**

This refers to the fact that norms, values and actions tend to be in operation long after the functions, activities and processes that initially created them disappear, thus generating so-called *slow fields of history*. These norms, values and actions exist though they have no apparent function, contributing to maintaining a type of behaviour long after the type of behaviour is functional or meaningful[2]. For sociologists and

---

[2] Asplund (1970: 55) refers to a similar phenomenon when he discusses Simmel. He points out that the norms that may have had a positive function during a historic phase become in a later phase dysfunctional.

historians it is important to determine whether norms and values have any function, or whether they are part of history's slow fields. By examining history's slow fields, it may be possible to provide better explanations for phenomena.

**Implicit Knowledge**. This is knowledge that is spread throughout an organization but not integrated.

**Information input overload**. This occurs when an individual, a team, an organization or a community receive more information than they can manage to process.

In a situation characterised by information input overload the following may occur (Miller, 1978: 123):

1. Designated tasks and responsibilities are left undone
2. Errors are made
3. Queues of information occur
4. Information is filtered out that should have been included
5. Abstract formulations are made when they should have been specific
6. Communication channels are overloaded, creating stress and tension in the system
7. Complex situations are shunned

8. Information is lumped together for processing

Each of the above eight points may result in a decrease in efficiency when the system is exposed to information input overload.

**Infostructure.** The infostructure concerns the processes that enable the development, transfer, analysis, storage, coordination and management of data, information and knowledge. The infostructure consists of eleven generic processes, as shown in Fig. 8 in this book. The eleven processes in the infostructure may be considered as nodes in a social network at different levels, for example team, organization, society, and region, all in the global space. Together, the eleven processes comprise the totality of the infostructure.

It may be said that the *info*structure has the same importance in the knowledge society as the *infra*structure had in the industrial society.

**Innovation.** Innovation is here understood as any idea, practice or material element, which is perceived as new for the person using it (Zaltman et al., 1973).

Ideas are seen as the smallest unit in the innovation process (Hamel, 2002; 2012). However, this refers to the ideas that are in process of development and not fully developed ideas. Before an idea can be characterized as innovative, it must prove to be beneficial to somebody, i.e. the market must accept the idea and apply it. Consequently, the creative process of innovation is here understood as the benefit it has for a market (Amabile, 1990; Johannessen, et al., 2001: 25). Thus, it is not sufficient that an idea is new for it to be considered an innovation. An idea may have a great degree of novelty, but if it is of no benefit to anybody in the market, then it has no innovative value.

**Knowledge**. The definition of knowledge used here is *the systematization and structuring of information for one or more goals or purposes.*

**Modularization**. An extreme fragmentation of the production process in the global knowledge economy. Production is fragmented and distributed according to the following logic: Costs – quality – competence – design – innovation.

**Modular flexibility.** The modulization of value creation. Modular flexibility may best be understood as the globalization of production processes, and extreme specialization of work processes with a focus on core processes.

**Necessary and sufficient conditions.** It may often be appropriate to divide conditions or premises into *necessary conditions* and *sufficient conditions*. Necessary conditions must be present to trigger an action, but these may not be sufficient. The sufficient conditions must also be present to trigger the action.

**North's action theory**[3]. This action theory may be expressed in the following statement: *People act on the basis of a system of rewards as expressed in the norms, values, rules and attitudes in the culture (the institutional framework)* (North, 1990; 1993). North's action theory is also consistent with Asplund's motivation theory (ref. Asplund's motivation theory).

---

[3] North's action theory is a term we use here based on North's research.

**Proposition**. This is an overarching hypothesis. It says something about the relationship between several variables. A proposition relates to a hypothesis in the same way the main research problem relates to research questions.

**Punctuation**. By punctuation (Bateson, 1972:292-293) a distinction is drawn between cause and effect; this is done with a clear motive in mind. A causality is thus created which does not actually exist in the real world, and one is then free to discuss the effects of this cause which has been created through a process of punctuation.

A sequence of a process is selected, and then bracketed. In this way, we de-limit what is punctuated from the rest of the process. Figuratively, we may imagine this as a circle that is divided into small pieces; one piece of the circle is then selected and folded out into a straight line. This results in the creation of an artificial beginning and end. This beginning and end of course cannot exist in a circle, but only through the process of punctuation.

**Social laws**. Social laws constitute a pattern of a unique type. They are systemic and connected to a system of knowledge, and cannot change without the facts they represent also being changed (Bunge, 1983; 1983a). The main differences between a statement of a law and other statements are:

1. Law statements are general.

2. Law statements are systemic, i.e. they are related to the established system of knowledge.

3. Law statements have been verified through many studies.

A pattern may be understood as variables that are stable over a specific period of time. A social law is created when an observer gains insight into the pattern. By gaining such insight, we can also predict parts of behaviour or at least develop a rough estimate within a short period of time.

Social laws are further related to specific social systems, both in time and space. However, this does not represent any objection to social laws, because this is also true of natural laws (although these have a longer time span and are of a more general nature).

**Social mechanism.** Robert Merton (1967) brought the notion of social mechanisms into sociology, although we can find rudiments of this in both Weber – with the Protestant ethic as an explanation for the emergence of capitalism in Europe – and in Durkheim, who uses society as an explanation for a rising suicide rate. For Merton, social mechanisms are the building blocks of *middle range theories*. He defines social mechanisms as *social processes having designated consequences for designated parts of the social structure* (Merton, 1968:43). In the 1980s and 1990s, Jon Elster developed a new notion of the role of social mechanisms in sociology (Elster, 1983;1989). Hedstrom and Swedberg write that, *the advancement of social theory calls for an analytical approach that systematically seeks to explicate the social mechanisms that generate and explain observed associations between events* (Hedstrøm & Swedberg, 1998:1).

It is one thing to point out connections between phenomena. It is something quite different to point out satisfactory explanations for these relationships, which is what social mechanisms accomplish. A social mechanism tells us what will happen, how it will happen and why it will happen (Bunge, 1967). Social mechanisms are primarily analytical constructs which cannot necessarily be observed; in other words, they are epistemological, not ontological. However, social mechanisms are observable in their consequences. An intention can be a social mechanism of action. We cannot observe an intention, but we can interpret it in light of the consequences manifested through an action. Preferences can also function as a social mechanism for economic behaviour. We cannot observe a person's preferences, but we can interpret them in the light of the behavioural consequences that manifest themselves. Social mechanisms are, understood in this way, analytical constructs, indicating connections between events (Hernes, 1998).

Bunge says: "... *a social mechanism is a process in a concrete system, such that it is capable of being about or preventing some change in the system as a whole or in some of its subsystems*" (Bunge, 1997:414). By 'social mechanism' here we mean those activities that promote/inhibit social processes in relation to a specific problem / phenomenon.

Material resources and technology are social mechanisms of the economic subsystem; power is a social mechanism of the political subsystem; fundamental norms and values are a social mechanism of the cultural subsystem; and human relationships are a social mechanism of the social subsystem. These system-specific social mechanisms interact with each other to achieve certain goals, maintain these systems, or to avoid certain undesirable conditions in the system or the outside world.

The difficulty of discovering social mechanisms and distinguishing them from processes may be partly explained by the fact that social mechanisms are also processes (Bunge, 1997:414). For the application of social mechanisms, see the Boudon-Coleman diagram.

**Social system**. From a systemic perspective, social systems can be conceptual or concrete. Theories and analytical models are examples of conceptual systems. Further, social systems are *composed of people and their artifacts* (Bunge, 1996:21). Social systems are held together (in systemic reasoning) by **dynamic social relations** (such as emotions, interpretations, norms, etc.) and **social actions** (such as, cooperation, solidarity, conflict and communication, etc.). None of the social actions have precedence in the systemic interpretation of social systems, such as conflict in the case of Marx, and solidarity in the case of Durkheim.

**Staccato-behaviour (erratic behaviour)**. If organizations introduce too many change processes in succession too quickly, a phenomenon may occur called "staccato-behaviour".

If an organization does not deal with this appropriately, it seems reasonable to assume that workers will become tired, burnt-out and de-motivated. Perhaps most damaging to business, employees will lose focus on their primary task - what the business is designed to do. In addition, businesses will often experience that this leads to an increasing degree of opportunistic behaviour (Ulrich, 2013a:260).

**Systemic thinking.** Systemic thinking makes a distinction between the epistemological sphere (Bunge, 1985), the ontological sphere (Bunge, 1983), the axiological sphere (Bunge, 1989, 1996) and the ethical sphere (Bunge, 1989). Systemic thinking makes a clear distinction between intention and behaviour. Intention is something that should be *understood*, while behaviour is something that should be *explained*. To understand an intention we must study the historical factors, situations and contexts, as well as the expectation mechanisms. Behaviour must be explained with respect to the context, relationships and situation it unfolds in. What implication does the distinction between intention and behavior have for the study of social systems?

Interpretation of meaning is an important part of the *intention aspect* in the distinction. Explanation and prediction become an essential part of the *behavioral aspect* of the distinction.

In systemic thinking it is the link between the interpretation of meaning and explanation, and prediction, which provides historical and social sciences with practical strength. By making a distinction between intention and behaviour, the historical and the social sciences are interpretive, explanatory and predictive projects. According to systemic thinking, many of the contradictions in the historical and social sciences spring from the fact that a distinction is not made between intention and behaviour. The problem of the historical and social sciences is that the actors who are studied have both intentions and they also exercise types of behaviour; however, this isn't problematic as long as we make a distinction between intention and behaviour. By simultaneously introducing the distinction between intention and behaviour, systemic thinking has made it possible to identify, for instance, partial explanations from each of two main epistemological positions, namely, the naturalists and anti-naturalists (Johannessen & Olaisen, 2005; 2006), and synthesize these explanations into new knowledge.

Systemic thinking emphasizes circular causal processes, also called *interactive causal processes*, in addition to linear causal processes (Johannessen, 1996; 1997). Systemic thinking argues that to understand objective social facts, one must examine the subjective aspects of these. In systemic thinking, objective social facts exist, but they are often more difficult to grasp than facts in the natural world, because social facts are often influenced by expectations, emotions, prejudices, ideology and economic and social interests. *"Aspect-seeing"* is thus a way of approaching these social facts.

Emergents are central to systemic thinking. A pattern behind the problem or phenomenon is always sought in systemic investigations. Patterns may be revealed by studying the underlying processes that constitute a phenomenon or problem, *and the search for pattern is what scientific research is all about* (Bunge, 1996:42).

According to systemic thinking it is a misconception to say that the facts are social constructions. The misunderstanding involves confusing our *concepts* concerning facts and our *hypotheses* about the facts together with the facts. Our concepts and hypotheses are mental constructs. The facts, however, are not mental constructs. Social need, for instance, is not a social fact; it is a mental construct of, for instance, starvation. Starvation is a social fact. Social need is a mental or social construction. Not being able to read is a social fact. Illiteracy is, however, a social construction.

A *symbol* should symbolize something, just as a *concept* should delineate something. A *hypothesis* should explain something or express something about relationships. A conceptual *model* should say something about the relationships between concepts. A *theory* should say something about relationships between propositions. Physical or social facts are untouched by all these mental constructions. That one can through constructs change social facts, or that social facts are changed as a social consequence of using constructs, is neither original nor new.

The aim of theoretical research, according to the systemic position, is the construction of systems, i.e. theories (Bunge, 1974: v). The order in systemic research is thus: Theory - Analysis - Synthesis.

In the methodological sphere, the systemic position has its main focus on relationships, both in terms of concrete things, ideas and knowledge. Consequently, systemic thinking encourages interdisciplinary and multidisciplinary approaches to problems or phenomena.

The systemic position thus attempts to bridge the gap between methodological individualism and methodological collectivism, which is considered the classic controversy in historical- and social sciences.

The perceptions that an observer has about social systems will influence his/her actions, regardless of whether the perceptions are true or fallacious. Systemic investigations start, therefore, writes Bunge *from individuals embedded in a society that preexists them and watch how their actions affect society and alter it* (Bunge, 1996:241). The study of social systems from a systemic perspective for these reasons always includes the triad: actors - observers - social systems.

The observer tries to uncover a system's composition, environment and structure. Then the actors' subjective perception of composition, environment and structure are examined. In other words, both the subjective and objective aspects are studied. When we wish to study changes in social systems, from a systemic point of view, we have to examine the social mechanisms (drivers) that influence changes; both internal and external social mechanisms must be identified. This study takes place within the four subsystems: the economic, political, cultural and relational. According to systemic thinking, social changes occur along seven axes:

1. As an *expectation* of new relationships, values, power constellations, technologies and distribution of material resources.
2. As a result of our *beliefs* (mental models) about relationships, values, power constellations, technical and material resources.
3. As a result of *psychological elements*, such as: irritation, crisis, discomfort, unsatisfactory life, unworthy life, loss of well-being, etc.
4. As a result of *communication* in and between systems.
5. As a result of an *understanding of connections* (contextual understanding).
6. As a result of learning and new *self-knowledge*.
7. As a result of *new ideas* and ways of thinking.

Historiography, from a systemic perspective, has one clear goal: to investigate what happened, where it happened, when it happened, how it happened, why it happened, and with what results.

Systemic assumptions related to historiography and social sciences may be expressed in the following (Bunge 1998:263):

a. The past has existed.
b. Parts of the past can be known.
c. Every uncovering of the past will be incomplete.
d. New data, techniques, and systemizations and structuring will reveal new aspects of the past.
e. Historical knowledge is developed through new data, discoveries, hypotheses and approaches.

In systemic thinking if changes are to take place, then the material will sometimes be given precedence; at other times, ideology, ideas and thinking are given precedence. In other contexts, there is a systemic link between the material and ideas that is needed to bring about changes. In such contexts, it is difficult and irrelevant to say what is the primary driver, i.e. the material or ideas; this would be on par with discussing what came first, the chicken or the egg.

The processes that drive social change, according to a systemic perspective, are the interaction between the economic, political, relational and cultural subsystems. In some situations, one of these four perspectives will prevail, whereas in others it will be one or more of the four subsystems that are the drivers of social change. In many cases, it is precisely the interaction between the four subsystems that leads to social changes.

In this context the systemic perspective may be described by saying that material conditions/energy, such as economic relationships, may provide the ground from which ideologies develop, but that these ideologies in return influence the development of the material. Whether material conditions / energy or ideology comes first is often determined by a historiographical punctuation process (Bateson, 1972:163).

The systemic perspective balances historical materialism and historical idealism. It assumes that overall social changes are the result of economic, political, social and cultural factors, in addition to the interaction between material conditions / energy and ideas. Furthermore, a systemic perspective views any society as being interwoven into its surroundings (Bunge, 1998: 275). When a historian considers a historical situation – such as the massacre in Van in April 1915 – from this perspective then he is trying *to throw light upon the internal working of a past culture and society* (Stone, 1979: 19).

The systemic position attempts to view the relevant event in a larger context, in order to find *the patterns which combine* (Bateson, 1972:273-274), because *change depends upon feedback loop* (Bateson, 1972:274). Bunge says about this position: *By placing the particular in a sequence, adopting a broad perspective the systemist overcomes the idiographic/nomothetic duality, ..., as well as the concomitant narrative/structural opposition* (Bunge 1998:275). This means, metaphorically, that the systemic researcher uses a microscope, telescope and a helicopter to investigate patterns over time.

Systemic research strategy is a *zig-zagging between the micro-meso and macro levels* (Bunge, 1998:277). Through a systemic research strategy the researcher has ample opportunities to use a Boudon-Coleman diagram.

Systemic thinking examines four types of changes[4].

Type I change concerns individuals who change history, such as Genghis Khan, Hitler, Stalin, Mao Zedong, etc.

Type II change concerns groups of people acting together who change history. Examples of Type II change include the invasion of the Roman Empire by peoples from the north; and the Ottoman expansion into the Balkans between the late 1400s and when the Ottoman Empire was pushed back partly due to nationalist liberation movements in the early 1900s.

Type III change include changes in history that are caused by

---

[4] The four types of changes are related to Bateson's (1972:279-309) work on different types of learning, especially those discussed in his article *Logical types of learning and communication*.

natural disasters, such as the volcanic eruption that destroyed Pompeii. Climate change may also be said to an example of a type III change.

Type IV change involves a total change in the way of thinking, such as the emergence of new religions, like Islam, or a new political ideology, such as Marxism.

The systemic researcher attempts to explore the relationship between the four types of changes. A single event is in itself not necessarily of special interest to the systemic researcher; rather, the focus is on the *system of events* of which the single event is a part.

All the social sciences are used in the systemic position to seek insight, understanding and to explain a phenomenon or problem.

**Tacit knowledge.** Knowledge that is difficult to communicate to others as information. It is also very difficult, if at all possible, to digitize.

**The knowledge-based perspective.** The knowledge-based perspective is defined here as creating, expanding and modifying internal and external competencies to promote what the organization is designed to do (Grant, 2003: 203).

**Theory.** Here understood as a system of propositions (Bunge, 1974: v).

# Index

## B

behaviour, 36, 48, 49, 52, 53, 55, 56, 57, 60, 62, 82, 83, 90, 91, 92, 94, 96, 97, 118, 119, 120, 128, 137, 142, 195, 196, 197, 201, 204, 210, 211, 213, 214
bias, 12, 14
Boudon-Coleman diagram, 195
Boudon-Colemandiagram, 221
Bunge, 30, 201, 212, 218, 220
bureaucratic, 166, 167, 168, 169

## C

capabilities, 168
causal, i, 36, 48, 50, 51, 52, 54, 56, 57, 58, 65, 66, 68, 69, 70, 71, 84, 142, 215
change, i, ii, 3, 4, 5, 7, 8, 10, 11, 12, 13, 14, 15, 16, 17, 18, 19, 21, 22, 23, 24, 25, 26, 27, 28, 29, 31, 35, 37, 39, 40, 41, 46, 57, 60, 61, 67, 69, 70, 72, 74, 79, 81, 82, 83, 84, 85, 86, 87, 89, 90, 92, 93, 94, 95, 96, 97, 98, 100, 103, 105, 106, 108, 113, 115, 130, 132, 134, 137, 153, 163, 164, 167, 168, 178, 183, 187, 196, 199, 200, 203, 209, 212, 213, 216, 219, 220, 221, 222
change processes, 163, 167
cluster, 109, 110, 111, 112, 113, 114, 115, 121, 122, 123, 124, 125, 126, 127, 128, 129, 130, 131, 133, 134, 135, 138, 139, 140, 141, 142
cognitive closeness, 80
communication, 161, 166, 174
competence, 151, 156, 157, 158, 159, 162, 163, 164, 165, 166, 168, 171, 173, 174, 175, 176, 177, 178, 179, 180
competition, 157, 172, 176, 177, 178
conceptual, 37, 40, 67, 70, 98, 213, 216
connections, 36, 50, 53, 58, 59, 64, 66, 67, 69, 126, 142, 167, 211, 218
context, 7, 8, 14, 20, 43, 52, 53, 54, 59, 64, 67, 84, 85, 93, 109, 114, 125, 135, 136, 143, 151, 158, 175, 177, 214, 220
control, 162
cooperation, 161, 169, 176, 177, 178, 180
culture, 48, 85, 93, 118, 178, 183, 185, 208, 220

customers, 150, 156, 165, 166, 167, 168, 178, 180

## D

distinction, 8, 37, 38, 39, 40, 43, 62, 88, 120, 122, 125, 128, 140, 143, 209, 214

## E

emergence, 153
Emergent, 200
empirical, 12, 30, 59, 61, 64, 65, 66, 68, 69, 71, 183
expectation, 6, 7, 26, 43, 53, 57, 90, 92, 97, 126, 201, 214, 218
explanations, 2, 36, 43, 45, 49, 58, 70, 71, 72, 121, 195, 198, 205, 211, 215

## F

feedback, 54, 55, 57, 87, 127, 135, 150, 201, 220
Feed-forward, 201
Framing, i, 11, 13, 14, 22, 23, 24, 28, 30, 32, 33, 93
front line, 156, 159, 165, 166, 168, 169, 176, 180
functional, ii, 52, 71, 92, 99, 122, 123, 124, 126, 130, 140, 163, 164, 178, 193, 204
functional areas, 163, 164

## G

global, 153, 157, 158, 159, 161, 162, 165, 167, 169, 171, 172, 173, 174, 175, 176, 177, 178, 179, 180, 181
global competence clusters, 165, 175, 180
globalization, 153, 154, 159, 167, 170, 172, 175

## I

idea, 161, 174, 176, 177
identity, 37, 38, 39, 41, 55, 56, 139, 158, 185
ideology, 81, 85, 90, 93, 215, 219, 220, 222
indicators, 62, 66, 121, 134, 138, 143
industrial society, 152, 153, 154, 155, 159, 165, 167, 177
industrial workers, 155, 172, 173
information, 3, 8, 11, 13, 14, 15, 16, 17, 18, 19, 20, 21, 23, 25, 26, 27, 28, 29, 60, 61, 82, 88, 96, 98, 99, 112, 119, 124, 126, 131, 134, 136, 138, 141, 150, 151, 152, 155, 156, 160, 161, 162, 164, 166, 167, 168, 169, 174, 176, 180, 181, 185, 194, 200, 202, 205, 206, 207, 222
infostructure, 155, 156, 159, 160, 161, 162, 163, 164, 165, 166, 171, 174, 175, 176, 180, 181, 182
Infostruktur, 206
infrastructure, 155, 161, 163, 164, 182
**infra**strukturen, 206
innovasjon, 193, 197, 198, 199, 203, 207, 208
innovasjoner, 204
innovation, 39, 69, 70, 71, 86, 90, 98, 100, 101, 113, 114, 115, 156, 161, 163, 165, 166, 167, 169, 171, 173, 174, 175, 176, 178, 193, 196, 197, 199, 203, 204, 206, 207
innovation price, 100
intensjon, 214, 215
intensjoner, 215
interconnected, 163

## J

justification, 13

## K

knowledge, iii, 18, 19, 23, 28, 43, 52, 60, 61, 62, 67, 70, 71, 72, 82, 88, 89, 109, 115, 116, 117, 119, 121, 129, 135, 136, 139, 140, 143, 149, 150, 151, 152, 153, 154, 155, 157, 158, 159, 160, 161, 162, 164, 165, 166, 167, 169, 171, 172, 174, 175, 176, 177, 179, 181, 182, 184, 187, 188, 189, 192, 193, 197, 198, 200, 202, 203, 204, 205, 206, 207, 209, 210, 215, 217, 218, 219, 222
knowledge economy, 153, 167, 175
knowledge organizations, 179
knowledge processes, 153, 155, 176
knowledge society, 152, 153, 154, 155, 158, 159, 162, 164, 166, 167, 169, 175, 177, 179, 182
knowledge-based organization, 150, 151, 160, 179

## L

law of requisite variety, 168
laws, 48, 56, 59, 60, 61, 67, 83, 84, 93, 118, 119, 120, 122, 129, 209, 210
levels, 24, 46, 117, 125, 161, 163, 165, 181, 195, 196, 202, 206, 221
linear, 43, 51, 53, 84, 139, 215

## M

macro, 44, 45, 46, 47, 116, 123, 147, 195, 221
management, 158, 160, 166, 180
micro, 44, 45, 46, 47, 116, 123, 195, 221
models, i, ii, 43, 54, 59, 63, 64, 65, 66, 67, 69, 70, 71, 80, 82, 90, 95, 96, 97, 140, 153, 213, 218

## N

normative expectations, 92, 93, 94, 98
normative legitimacy, 80
normatively closed, 80
norms, 37, 81, 84, 85, 90, 93, 95, 98, 131, 141, 142, 197, 204, 208, 212, 213
Norths handlingsteori, 208

## O

OECD, 203
opportunity, 8, 11, 12, 162, 201
organization, 150, 151, 161, 162, 165, 168, 169, 171
organizational learning, 168
organizations, 150, 156, 158, 159, 160, 162, 165, 166, 168, 177, 181, 182
organize, 13

## P

patterns, 48, 49, 56, 58, 59, 60, 61, 67, 81, 96, 97, 118, 119, 120, 135, 138, 142, 202, 220
performance, 150
perspective, ii, 17, 18, 32, 49, 60, 68, 80, 82, 83, 84, 86, 87, 89, 92, 94, 95, 109, 115, 119, 120, 129, 136, 184, 195, 199, 212, 217, 218, 219, 220, 221, 222
phenomenon, 13, 44, 47, 62, 63, 64, 65, 67, 68, 69, 70, 71, 72, 82, 119, 131, 133, 135, 136, 137, 139, 142, 143, 155, 159, 196, 204, 212, 213, 215, 222
possibility, 3, 5, 6, 8, 9, 10, 68, 92, 162
processes, i, 3, 5, 10, 12, 33, 36, 39, 40, 41, 46, 47, 50, 51, 52, 54, 55, 56, 57, 58, 59, 62, 67, 71, 84, 85, 87, 96, 97, 112, 116, 124, 134, 136,

138, 139, 140, 141, 142, 150, 152, 155, 156, 157, 158, 159, 160, 161, 162, 163, 164, 166, 167, 168, 169, 170, 175, 179, 180, 181, 196, 197, 200, 203, 204, 206, 208, 211, 212, 213, 215, 216, 219
productivity, 158, 176
prospect theory, 2, 3, 5, 6, 7, 9, 13, 14, 15, 17, 27, 30

## R

reference point, 6, 9, 14, 15
reflection effect, 7, 8, 11, 23
relations, i, 30, 37, 39, 41, 46, 47, 48, 60, 65, 84, 90, 92, 93, 95, 98, 116, 124, 131, 132, 135, 197, 213
resistance, 2, 3, 7, 8, 11, 15, 18, 22, 23, 26, 27, 29, 91
responsibility, 158

## S

service, 164, 166, 169
social, i, 30, 35, 36, 37, 38, 39, 40, 41, 42, 43, 44, 45, 46, 47, 48, 49, 50, 51, 52, 53, 54, 55, 56, 58, 59, 60, 61, 63, 65, 67, 71, 72, 75, 76, 80, 82, 83, 84, 85, 86, 89, 90, 91, 92, 93, 94, 95, 96, 101, 110, 117, 118, 119, 120, 121, 122, 127, 129, 131, 137, 139, 155, 156, 157, 158, 160, 161, 162, 163, 164, 172, 175, 178, 179, 181, 194, 196, 197, 202, 203, 206, 210, 211, 212, 214, 215, 216, 217, 218, 219, 220, 222
social mechanisms, i, 35, 36, 37, 41, 42, 43, 46, 47, 48, 51, 52, 53, 54, 56, 58, 59, 67, 68, 71, 72, 76, 86, 110, 131, 160, 196, 197, 210, 211, 212, 218
stability, 37, 39, 40, 41, 81, 83, 86, 95, 114, 167, 178, 203
stakkato-atferd, 213
strategi, 195, 221
strategisk, 213
*strategiske*, 213
**Structure**, 73, 76, 77, 104, 105, 106, 124, 131, 132, 139, 146
suppliers, 156, 166, 168
system, 14, 29, 37, 38, 39, 40, 41, 44, 47, 48, 52, 53, 56, 57, 59, 60, 61, 62, 64, 69, 71, 72, 80, 81, 83, 84, 86, 87, 88, 90, 91, 92, 93, 96, 98, 99, 100, 109, 110, 112, 116, 117, 122, 125, 132, 133, 134, 137, 142, 143, 151, 156, 164, 168, 173, 176, 177, 178, 181, 182, 183, 196, 197, 198, 200, 205, 206, 208, 209, 210, 212, 217, 222, 223
systemic thinking, 37, 40, 110, 117, 137, 197, 214, 215, 216, 217, 218, 219

## T

Theory, i, 2, 75, 76, 77, 103, 104, 148, 188, 192, 217, 223

## U

Ulrich. Se
uncertain, 11, 23
understand, 13, 44, 49, 58, 64, 81, 83, 84, 89, 94, 96, 112, 116, 125, 151, 160, 169, 214, 215

## V

value, 152, 153, 155, 156, 157, 158, 159, 160, 162, 166, 167, 169, 170, 174, 175, 177, 178, 179, 181, 182

## Ø

## THE AUTHOR

Jon-Arild Johannessen holds a Master of Science from Oslo University in History. He holds a Ph.D. from Stockholm University in Systemic thinking. He is currently professor (full) in Leadership, at Kristiania University College, Oslo and Nord University, Norway. He has been professor (full) in Innovation, at Syd-danske University, Denmark. He has been professor (full) in Management at The Arctic University, Norway. At Bodø Graduate School of Business, Norway he had a professorship (full) in Information management At Norwegian School of

Management he has been professor in Knowledge Management.

www.ingramcontent.com/pod-product-compliance
Lightning Source LLC
Chambersburg PA
CBHW070236190526
45169CB00001B/198